where the heart
longs to go

where the heart longs to go

a new image for pastoral ministry

Thad Rutter Jr.

UPPER
ROOM BOOKS
NASHVILLE

Where the Heart Longs to Go
© 1998 by Thad Rutter Jr.
All rights reserved.

The Upper Room Website: http.://www.upperroom.org

Art direction: Michele Wetherbee
Interior design and layout: Ellisor Design
First printing: January 1998

Library of Congress Cataloging-in-Publication Data
Rutter, Thad, 1937–
   Where the heart longs to go: a new image for pastoral ministry / Thad Rutter.
       p. cm.
   Originally presented as the author's thesis (Doctor of Ministry).
   ISBN 0-8358-0849-1
   1. Clergy—Religious life. 2. Contemplation. 3. Pastoral theology. 4. United Methodist Church (U.S.)—Clergy—Religious life. 5. Spiritual life—United Methodist Church (U.S.) 6. Pastoral theology—United Methodist Church (U.S.) I. Title.
BV4011.6.R88 1998   97-18090
248.3 ' 4—DC21   CIP

To Jack

who taught me to trust
what God gives me to see
and calls me to be and do

CONTENTS

FOREWORD

This is an important book. It comes from the prayerful, raw, and immediate experience of a faithful pastor's long years in parish ministry. It has the authenticity that comes from living all the joys and struggles of that ministry in prayer and in integrity. I want also to mention the "strange blessings" (his words) that he has further received since the completion of this work: a tornado that totally destroyed his church and the parsonage ten seconds after he had escaped into the basement to save his life and a life-threatening illness, around the same time, from which he is now recovering. Thad wears his scars and his blessings quietly, thoughtfully, and prayerfully; United Methodists are graced to have him among their pastors.

But the import of this book does not rest only on the faithfulness of the author. It is a significant contribution to the work of pastoral ministry. It is grounded solidly in scripture, theology, and especially the Wesleyan "master model"—a metaphor for the work of pastoral ministry that can be widely applied to various aspects of ministry. The metaphor is that of the minister as spiritual leader, whose own life of contemplative prayer is the constantly renewing and vital spring of who he/she fundamentally is and what he/she actually does each day in ministry.

In developing this approach Thad articulates a number of important insights from others and from his own experience. I am particularly drawn to his description of the "language of the Spirit"—expressed in poetry, metaphor, shared silence, and intimacy—that becomes a way to recognize and share the "divine longing in the heart" for the presence of God. It has long been recognized that the church is tragically often the last place people are comfortable sharing this most intimate area of their lives. But Thad does even more than describe the spiritual life eloquently and sensitively; he shares research and illustrates a process for awakening people to "God's vast giveaway."

Thad's research indicates various ways in which people are awakened in their lives and in the church to their longing and to the Presence. He then articulates a way of being that can evoke spiritual conversation, along with specific descriptions of theological context, settings, questions, and responses for the conversation. It seems to me that this approach can be more than a part of one's ministry; it can be adapted and applied throughout the pastor's work and is equally relevant to lay ministries. As Eugene Peterson wrote, "Say the Word accurately, say the Name personally"—so Thad does, in this witness which is at the same time profound and practically valuable for ministry.

—John Biersdorf

EXPRESSIONS OF GRATITUDE

I have many wonderful thoughts and feelings upon completion of this book. One of the predominant feelings is gratitude to the people who have played a part in its content. First, I want to thank the following members of Aldersgate United Methodist Church, who were interview participants: Bob Reimer, Evaline Keller, Kathi Canfield, Mary Dove, Wendy Garrett, Carol Pope, Judi Wilger, Karen Gravenkamp, Bobbie Langlois, Barb Reimer, Mary Thomsen, Barb Eddy, Marion Tuttle, Faye Iverson, Jan Gravenkamp, Pat Brandt, Lynn Rutter, Sheila Niggermeier, Rachel Hadley, and Lori Sistler. These people shared with me the deep treasures of their hearts. Their gift to me is humbling.

I want to thank Rev. Gerry Harrison, Rev. Colleen Bennker, and Rev. "Arv" Arveson, who gave their thoughtful responses to this work as a doctor of ministry dissertation.

I want to thank Dr. Wayne Fehr and Rev. Larry Warren, who have informed and formed my mind and heart through sharing prayer.

I want to thank Rev. George Donigian, the editor at the Upper Room with whom I worked. I have deeply appreciated his counsel, affirmation, and friendship.

I want to express a bundle of thank-yous to my wife, Lynn, who read, reread, edited, reedited, typed, and retyped this manuscript for publication.

Finally I want to thank Dr. John Biersdorf, who is both a teacher and friend. He, more than any other, affirmed and mentored me in my call to pastoral ministry rooted in contemplative prayer.

NAMING THE QUESTION OF THIS QUEST

As Joseph Campbell was so fond of saying, the whole point and meaning of life is to discover and follow your bliss. And this is ours—to attend to the presence of God in community and in solitude, in action and reception, in pain and in happiness, in our doing and in our being.[1]
—JOHN BIERSDORF

The "ours" to whom John Biersdorf refers in this quote from a *Haelen* article (Summer 1989) are ministers called to contemplative prayer. I have come to see that I am one with such a call. Not everyone is called to the inner work of a contemplative, but all Christians are called to face and make choices about the often hidden desires and intentions of their hearts. Christian wholeness and Christlike living depend upon such inner awareness. Dr. Biersdorf goes on to state the struggle and a key question that those called to contemplative prayer carry:

> That [tending to the presence of God] is what drew us into ministry. We experienced the call of God, church and heart in this way. And we still do. Even when things are at their worst, after crying out in pain, we come back to it.

And herein lies the exquisitely poignant theological question, *Can one understand and live ministry in this way?*[2] (*Italics mine.*)

This book is the story of my addressing Dr. Biersdorf's question. It really is the story of my facing, understanding, and learning to be embraced by a deep ache in my heart. The ache is my longing for God that is borne of God's longing for me.

In his article, Dr. Biersdorf discusses the immense challenge pastors, including myself, have in maintaining an authentic spiritual life and discipline in the face of parish life. Dr. Biersdorf does not, however, play "ain't it awful" in relationship to the church. He counsels, "We have to begin with ourselves," and offers this promising confession with which so many of us can identify:

> I never reach the point where I am exempt from the raw vulnerability of confessing my powerlessness over my life and circumstances, my evasions of intimacy with myself, others and God, and the tough work of surrendering it all to God and living in faith. I understand myself as a recovering co-dependent. But in a larger sense, I and we all are recovering "human doings" instead of human beings, each with our particular chronic and temporary ways of avoiding God.[3]

"Beginning with myself" is what I have done in this book. It is the story of my pursuit of Dr. Biersdorf's question by asking, "What are the ways a local church pastor can awaken people to God's longing for them and their longing for God?" It is the story of my uncovering my own longing for God and my growth in the understanding of this longing through exploration of scripture, the life and thought of John Wesley (I am United Methodist), and several contemporary writers. The book is also an account of the ways people from the church I served in Milwaukee awakened to God, which I explored through an interview process. Finally this book includes reflections on what it means for a local church pastor to live a life and ministry rooted in contemplative prayer.

Although this book is about my learning to live my contemplative call in ministry, I believe it is for any Christian who struggles to tend to God and to maintain an authentic spiritual life in a church and world that threatens to turn all of us into "human doings." My hope is that the stories I tell of my inner and outer quest to respond to God's longing for me and mine for God will awaken the same in you.

MY OWN AWAKENING

Moving through the heart of every person in the universe is a silent cry that yearns for understanding. This silent cry is an ache for God, searching to be named. It is everybody's ache. It is immensely deep.[1]

—MACRINA WIEDERKEHR
A TREE FULL OF ANGELS

The moment I first awakened to God's longing for me is one I will always cherish. It occurred some thirty-three years ago on a winter evening when I was a first-year graduate student in clinical psychology. I had become interested in the writings of Paul Tillich through a religion course my senior year in college and had purchased his book of sermons *The Shaking of the Foundations*. I read a sermon each night as a devotional.

I was attracted to the book especially because of its title. When I was fourteen my foundations were traumatically shaken. I was severely injured in an auto accident in which two people were killed. The guilt and shame I experienced as an "unworthy" (or so I thought) survivor scarred me, and I carried deep doubt about my self-worth. The guilt and shame also made me receptive to Tillich's description of divine grace in his sermon, "You Are Accepted": "Sometimes at that moment a wave of light breaks into our darkness, and it is as though a voice were saying: 'You are accepted. *You are accepted*, accepted by that which is greater than you, and the name of which you do not know.'"[2]

I put the book down. Tears came to my eyes. Unspeakable peace came into my heart. "You are accepted. You are accepted, accepted by that which is greater than you." My heart uttered in a quiet, ecstatic way, *I can't believe this is true.* But of course it was. I had awakened to the fact that I had been all my life, was at that moment, and always would be held in God's amazing grace.

That life-altering experience led me to seminary the following year. As I look back upon it now, I feel this experience with the writings of Tillich was the beginning of my faith journey, which has included thirty-three years of pastoral ministry. And it was the beginning of my realization of God's longing for me.

Only in the past seven years have I come to realize that not only does God long for me, but I have a deep, often overlooked, longing for God. Why did it take me so long to recognize and awaken to this inner holy longing? For most of the years of my ministry (the sixties through the mid-eighties), spirituality was held suspect. My awakening to my heart's divine longing corresponds with the rebirth of things spiritual. This awakening occurred for me gradually, beginning in March 1990. Looking back on it, I feel I went through three stages I have called respectively Quiet Crisis, Inner Realization, and Outer Quest.

Quiet Crisis

Though *quiet crisis* seems an odd term, it is an apt description of this period in my life. What happened was both quiet and of crisis proportions. I didn't lose my job, marriage, or anything else of significant value. On the surface, all appeared normal: I showed up where I needed to and did what I was supposed to do as a pastor. But that normal functioning belied a deep inner dysfunctioning that I might have lived with to my grave. I experienced it as an underlying dissatisfaction and emptiness in my life and ministry. This inner unrest led me to seek psychological counseling, and it was my counselor who named for me what lay at the core of my pain. One day, after listening to me describe my work as a pastor for about a half hour, in a gentle, matter-of-fact way, she observed, "Thad, you are in a crisis in your relationship to God's movement in your life."

It was a grace-filled moment for me, full of a mysterious and undergirding peace. But it was grace and peace with a grave challenge. This astute observer of my heart gave me the good news that God, indeed, was moving in my heart and the bad news that I was not paying attention to that movement.

The moment she spoke, I knew my counselor was absolutely correct, but I also knew my condition wasn't due to spiritual neglect. In my opinion, I was seriously tending to my work as pastor and to my spirituality. The problem was that I was making it *my* work and *my* spirituality. In that counselor's office, I experienced the truth of spiritual writer James Finley's statement: "God hates your spirituality and loves you."

The "quiet crisis" created by this realization became the opportunity of my lifetime. I slowly began to let God's spirit show me the kind of spirituality and pastoring God intended for me. This led to the second stage.

Inner Realization

I was guided to this "inner realization" by James Finley in his book *The Awakening Call*. In the book's introduction, Finley contends that a call to contemplative prayer can come to anyone: teachers, homemakers, businesspeople, physicians, laborers, and spiritual leaders. Finley then discusses the nature of contemplative prayer and helps the reader discern whether he or she has received such a call.

I still can recall quite vividly spending an hour each morning slowly reading small portions of Finley's book. This reading was an experience of prayer as I found myself being drawn inwardly to this long-overlooked core desire that lived in my heart. I slowly came to the realization that my heart longed to know God, live in God's presence, and have God's presence live in me. The Holy Spirit, through Finley's writings, awakened me to see that God was guiding me to relate to and to serve God through the call of contemplative prayer.

To me even now there is something unheroic about this inner realization. To be frank, I have always longed for a passion that would lead me to prophetic deeds of renown—acts that would tilt history in God's direction on a grand scale. To quietly let God lead me to see what lies at the core of my heart and who I am appears quite irrelevant and unproductive from a certain perspective. But in the fall of 1990, as I spent that hour reading *The Awakening Call*, I realized I was being given my bliss. That bliss was my desire to inwardly tend to and outwardly live in the presence of God.

Outer Quest

It seems that once God answers one set of questions, God is always ready to give us a brand-new set. I felt God had showed me that my call in ministry was rooted in contemplative prayer. I now found myself asking, *Can I have a pastoral ministry rooted in contemplative prayer? If so, what is its nature? What are my pastoral role and tasks with such a call?*

These questions led me to two new ventures in pastoral ministry. The first was to devise an interview process. The questions for that process grew from my own inner realization of God's presence and call in my life. In this first venture, I sat down individually with thirteen people from my church. I asked them to get in touch with their life journeys and the times in their lives when they felt close to God. (The full interview process is included in the Appendix.)

All thirteen responded most enthusiastically to the interviews. I accumulated pages of notes, filled with insights and indescribable treasures about these people. The results of this interview showed me that a venture in ministry rooted in contemplative prayer had a place in parish life. Clearly the process had struck a chord with these people.

I puzzled for a couple of months at what lay at the core of the enthusiastic response engendered by the interviews. One answer was rather apparent: I had invited people to get in touch with and share their life stories. I came to see that aspect as an important offering of a ministry rooted in contemplative prayer, for part of the contemplative experience is the profound sense of knowing that God hears and regards one's experiences. But it was Macrina Wiederkehr's speaking of "a silent cry that yearns for understanding," which helped me realize the second thing that had occurred, the core thing: I had led people to touch, share, and legitimize their ache for God.

This realization led me to another question and my second new venture in ministry. I believe God gave me this second question as I worked through the preceding interview process. The question was this: *What are the ways a local church pastor can awaken people to God's longing for them and their longing for God?* I sought answers to my question in the wisdom of scripture, in the wisdom of John Wesley, in the wisdom of contemporary spiritual writers, and in my own experiences in pastoral ministry. I also devised a second interview process in which I interviewed eighteen people in my parish to discover the ways they had awakened to God's longing for them and their longing for God. The pages of this book contain my discoveries from all these sources, as well as what these discoveries have meant to my life and ministry. It has been a holy revelation for me, and I hope it may be one for you as well.

THE LONGING IN LIGHT OF SCRIPTURE

O God, you are my God, I seek you,
my soul thirsts for you;
my flesh faints for you,
as in a dry and weary land where there is no water.
So I have looked upon you in the sanctuary,
beholding your power and glory.
Because your steadfast love is better than life,
my lips will praise you.
So I will bless you as long as I live;
I will lift up my hands and call on your name.
—PSALM 63:1-4

Once I had known the divine longing, both personally and through the affirmations of my parishioners, I decided to investigate what scripture had to say about it. I wanted to glean all the biblical wisdom and knowledge I could about the nature of God's longing for us and the human heart's longing for God.

I didn't have to look far. The Bible reveals immediately—that is, in the first three chapters of Genesis—four sentinel truths about God and the human heart's longing for God. (A fifth truth follows later in scripture.) I call these "sentinel" truths because the rest of the biblical drama flows from the truths about God and human nature revealed in these early chapters of Genesis.

The First Sentinel Truth

Genesis opens with a number of revelations, one of which describes the nature of the divine longing. "In the beginning...God created" (Gen. 1:1). These words challenge us to a mental transformation. We must turn from the mind-set that says we initiate our relationship with God. The truth we discover in the first verse of Genesis confirms that before we "thought" of God, God thought of us—and willed us into being. Before we loved God, God loved us. Before we searched for God, God was searching for us. Before we longed for God, God was longing for us.

In Rueben Job and Norman Shawchuck's *Guide to Prayer for Ministers and Other Servants*, the spiritual writer John Dunne underscored this truth, saying that to embrace it we must let our hearts reveal truths that our minds do not see.

> "There is a dream dreaming us," a Bushman once told Laurens Van der Post. We are part of a dream, according to this, part of a vision. What is more, we can become aware of it. . . . We can indeed come to a sense of being dreamed, being seen, being known. Our minds' desire is to know, to understand; but our heart's desire is intimacy, to be known, to be understood. To see God with our mind would be to know God, to understand God; but to see God with our heart would be to have a sense of being known by God, of being understood by God.[1]

This sentinel truth is present in all the Bible's theophanies:

Abram's call—"Now the Lord said to Abram . . ." (Gen. 12:1);
Moses at the burning bush—"The angel of the Lord appeared
to [Moses] in a flame of fire out of a bush" (Exod. 3:2); Samuel
asleep in the sanctuary—"Then the Lord called, 'Samuel!
Samuel!'" (1 Sam. 3:4); grieving Isaiah in the temple—"In the
year that King Uzziah died, I saw the Lord sitting on a throne,
high and lofty" (Isa. 6:1); Jeremiah, disclosing the nature of his
call—"Before I formed you in the womb I knew you, and
before you were born I consecrated you; I appointed you a
prophet to the nations" (Jer. 1:5); the Annunciation—"The
angel said to her, 'The Holy Spirit will come upon you, and
the power of the Most High will overshadow you; therefore
the child to be born will be holy; he will be called Son of
God'" (Luke 1:35); and finally the disciples being met by the
risen Lord Jesus—"When it was evening on that day...and the
doors of the house where the disciples had met were locked
for fear of the Jews, Jesus came and stood among them and
said, 'Peace be with you'" (John 20:19).

Grasping God's initiative changes the origin and nature of
my question of the way one awakens to the divine longing. I
often entertained the notion that my curiosity about God's
pursuit of us had arisen from my professional training and my
spiritual acuteness. The Bible jarred me into the awareness that
quests for God don't originate with the human mind and heart
but with God. Again, before we seek God, God has been seeking us. Before we inquire of God, God has been inquiring of
us. Before we know God, God knows us through and through.
Before we long for God, God longs for us.

O Lord, you have searched me and known me.
You know when I sit down and when I rise up;
    you discern my thoughts from far away.

> You search out my path and my lying down,
>   and are acquainted with all my ways.
> Even before a word is on my tongue,
>   O Lord, you know it completely.
> You hem me in, behind and before,
>   and lay your hand upon me.
> Such knowledge is too wonderful for me;
>   it is so high that I cannot attain it. (Ps. 139:1-6)

The Bible reminds me that before my question was an inquiry of my heart, it was a gift to my heart. The Bible's first sentinel truth is that the perspectives, the awakenings, the longings, the inquiries, and the love that bring life and meaning are gifts from God. As John Dunne pointed out, they are dreams we have been given to dream by the Holy One who dreams us, confronts us, guides us, and always gives us life abundant. Quite often we are unaware of the gifts the divine Giver has given us. It does not matter, for our unawareness of the Giver does not blunt God's awareness of us and God's intention to give us the gifts we need for our well-being.

The Second Sentinel Truth

The second sentinel truth revealed in Genesis 1-2 explains the nature of our desire for God:

> So God created humankind in his image, in the image of God he created them; male and female he created them (Gen. 1:27).

> Then the Lord God formed man from the dust of the ground, and breathed into his nostrils the breath of life; and the man became a living being (Gen. 2:7).

From the beginning the human heart's deepest desire has been to know intimately and be known by God. From this deep desire comes awareness of who God is, who we are, and the purpose for our lives. James Finley awakens prayerful appreciation for what the Genesis writer expressed in these two passages: "We close our eyes in prayer and open them in the pristine moment of creation. We open our eyes to find God,...hands still smeared with clay, hovering over us, breathing into us...divine life, smiling to see in us a reflection of [God's] self."[2]

When prayer opens our eyes, we realize we are creations of a loving, purposeful Creator. When prayer opens our eyes, we understand how utterly dependent we are upon the divine breath that breathes us continually into being. When prayer opens our eyes, we realize God's longing for us has imparted in the core place of our hearts a longing for God. This longing has been given to each human being at birth.

The Interpreter's Dictionary of the Bible points out that the word *heart* has several meanings in Hebrew. It is a metaphor that points to "the seat of psychic life," "the point of contact with God," and "the equivalent of the personality." When I speak of the human heart's longing for God as implied in Genesis, I am speaking primarily of the second meaning: "the point of contact with God." Expanding on this, *The Interpreter's Dictionary* says, "The heart, as the innermost spring of the human personality, is directly open to God and subject to [God's] influence. The heart speaks to God (Ps. 27:8) and trusts God (Ps. 28:7); the word of God dwells in it (Deut. 30:14); and there faith takes its rise (Rom. 10:10)."[3]

The second sentinel truth is that from God's longing for us flows the human heart's longing for God. This God-created longing is deep and all defining. It serves as our point of contact with God, as well as our point of contact with ourselves,

others, and our world. Through that part of us we know who
God is, who we are, and the purpose for our living. To turn
from this core truth of our hearts is to experience terrifying
dislocation and disorientation.

The Third Sentinel Truth

Genesis 3, the story of the Fall, reveals the third sentinel truth.
This is an account of loss—tremendous and irreplaceable loss
to the human heart.

Before looking at this story, I want to say a word about the
language and forms that the biblical writers employed to reveal
this core truth of the human heart. I believe the story is one that
God revealed to their hearts about the human heart. I think we
should approach the story of the Fall for what it is: a divinely
inspired vision of the way things are between God and us.

The setting is a garden of pristine harmony, beauty, and
abundance. Blending in with the garden's beauty is a serpent. It
seems to belong there, in that we are told, "The serpent was
more crafty than any other wild animal that the Lord God had
made" (Gen. 3:1). In this land where once it was natural for
animals and people to talk, the serpent engages the mother of
humankind in a conversation. Through a series of subtle questions, the serpent suggests that the woman consider how excit-
ing and enhancing it would be to see all God sees and know all
God knows.

Earlier in the story, God had given the woman and man
but one rule: Avoid the fruit of the tree of the knowledge of
good and evil, for it would bring them death. But that was
then—this was now. The tree was right before the woman's
eyes; God's presence was not. The desire to know what God
knew simply overwhelmed her desire for God. She could not
resist the temptation to discover what lay beyond God's pres-

ence and intention for her life, for that is what the fruit of God's powers promised. So she ate.

The fruit initially drugged the woman into a high that she was eager to share with her companion. He too ate.

Soon they discovered that the serpent's poison and this tasty fruit had transported their consciousness to a land beyond the bounds of God's love. They experienced what God foretold: They saw their own nakedness before the reality of death. The sight filled them with terror and shame. Earlier God's love adorned their nakedness. Earlier their vulnerability toward God and each other was a gift of which they were unashamed (see Gen. 2:25). Now their need for God and each other became an occasion of unbearable fear and remorse. To survive they hurriedly covered their desire for God's presence and for each other with fig leaves.

The snake had deceived them, and now all they could do was pretend. They pretended to be something God never intended them to be—Godlike without God! But as the story and the rest of the Bible make clear, their ache for God never really left them. Yet by turning away from God, they had become too afraid to let God touch them.

This indeed is a story of unspeakable loss, beginning with the loss of our natural trust in and awareness of God. As God lovingly approached the man and woman simply to be with them, they hid themselves in the trees. Their shame in the presence of God blinded them.

Then the man and woman lost awareness of their hearts' longing for God. Their betrayal of God's love separated their consciousness from the core and defining desire of their hearts.

The final loss was that of identity. The man and woman clothed themselves in fig leaves (see Gen. 3:7). They no longer saw and embraced their true identity as naked, vulnerable human beings in constant need of holy love.

We have lost our awareness of God's presence and purpose for us. We have lost our awareness of our heart's deepest longing. And we have lost the sense of who we really are: God's naked, yet much-loved children. A death of the spirit has paralyzed our hearts. This death that is of our making, not God's, is called "original sin," and there is no known human cure. The third sentinel truth of the Genesis story is that we have turned away from and lost the primary gift of life—our longing for God, in which we discover our identity and purpose for living. This loss is tragedy of the highest and deepest order, and the loss is compounded by the fourth sentinel truth of Genesis.

The Fourth Sentinel Truth

We have seen the depth of our loss in the first three truths. The fourth sentinel truth tells us that it is impossible for us to reverse the consequences of violating God's command to live in and desire God's love. "[God] drove [them] out…; and at the east of the garden of Eden he placed the cherubim, and a sword flaming and turning to guard the way to the tree of life" (Gen. 3:24). We cannot mend or restore what was severed. Adam and Eve and all their children carry with them their longing for God, which was such a natural part of them when they were at home in the garden. Their longing, however, cannot and will not make it so.

To return to my original question: *What are the ways a local church pastor can awaken people to respond to God's longing for them and their longing for God?* The Genesis story's first two sentinel truths affirm the legitimacy and importance of the question. They tell us that to live in God's longing for us and our longing for God is the key to life. The story's last two sentinel truths remind this pastor that "answers" to his question lie outside his competency. They aren't his to figure out or devise, because he has fallen away from both God's longing for him and his heart's longing for God.

That, however, is certainly not all the Bible has to say in answer to this question.

The Fifth Sentinel Truth

We turn now to the New Testament, which discloses this truth throughout but most succinctly through Paul in Romans 7–8. Paul picks up where the Genesis story of the Fall ends. With trust, openness, and courage Paul tells his readers the kind of conflict and disarray he carries in his heart:

> So I find it to be a law that when I want to do what is good, evil lies close at hand. For I delight in the law of God in my inmost self, but I see in my members another law at war with the law of my mind, making me captive to the law of sin that dwells in my members. Wretched man that I am! Who will rescue me from this body of death? (Rom. 7:21-24)

Paul writes like a condemned man, which he in fact is. He knows he is condemned to live a false existence of self-love, while at the same time he knows his "inmost self" longs to delight in the law of God's love.

In answer to my question, Paul, this earliest of Christian spiritual leaders, seems to be saying that one begins by confronting the betrayal and pretenses that surround and drive one's life: "Face the puzzling resistance to loving God that your heart carries. Feel the pain and the conflict in your avoiding and fleeing the deep desire of your heart. Dare to disclose openly the way it is with you. Lead by example."

But this early spiritual guide who knew despair and wrote

of it openly also says, "Don't live in despair! Live in belief and trust! Trust God enough to let out your heart's most nagging, unresolved question: 'Who will rescue me from this body of death?'" Surprisingly, Paul finds that his daring to feel and disclose this question is what awakens him to God's response to him: "Thanks be to God through Jesus Christ our Lord!" (Rom. 7:25).

Paul, our scriptural pastor, encourages our hearts to know, "There is therefore now no condemnation for those who are in Christ Jesus. For the law of the Spirit of life in Christ Jesus has set you free from the law of sin and of death" (Rom. 8:1-2).

Paul, by personal confession and proclamation, awakens us to see that our hearts are not condemned to an endless cycle of narcissistic self-love. Paul, by personal story, gives us the pastoral word that when our hearts turned from God, God did not turn from us. In Christ, the betrayer is given back the very thing that is betrayed. In Christ, the betrayer becomes once again the faithful child seeking the love of a parent. The treasured, lost longing comes back to us not as a prize attained but as a gift given. I hear Paul saying, "Begin your quest of awakening with an acknowledgment of your need for a merciful awakening, and trust that God longs to give you what you need."

Paul honors my question's legitimacy, yet at the same time he offers no methods. Instead he offers his own weakness and inadequacies and his faith in the companionship, the mercy, the healing, and the guidance of Christ. Paul reminds us that when we trust our belief that Christ desires to live in us and others—in the same way Christ has been living in Paul—we will be showed the ways that a spiritual leader, or anyone else, can awaken people to respond to God's longing for them and their longing for God.

This is the fifth sentinel truth that emerges from scripture: In the grace and mercy of Christ Jesus, God has restored to the human heart its lost longing for God. God is the Awakener who awakens!

As revealed in the five sentinel truths, the Gospels and all the Christian scriptures give this response to my question: The way to awaken people to respond to God's longing for them and their longing for God is to believe that from the beginning, now, and forevermore, God longs for us. Then believe that our God-given nature is to long for God. That is the original blessing we have forsaken, and that is the reason the human heart knows a primordial despair and loneliness.

Finally, believe that God in Jesus Christ has restored the holy longing which we have lost. Let that belief define who you are and what you are about.

In response to this knowledge, be in holy communion and service with Christ through his Body, the church. The New Testament leads us to a community of believers. Acts 2:42 pinpoints places to seek his light:

"They devoted themselves"—approach this quest with a devoted, committed heart;

"to the apostles' teaching"—he is known in scripture stories about him;

"and fellowship"—he is known in the eyes of fellow believers;

"to the breaking of bread"—he is known in his holy meal

"and the prayers"—he is known in our heart's deepest longing.

The ways a pastor can awaken people to the divine longing are to be lodged in Christ and revealed in his sacramental community, the church.

THE LONGING IN UNITED METHODIST HERITAGE

The beauty of holiness, of that inward [one] of the heart which is renewed after the image of God, cannot but strike every eye which God hath opened, every enlightened understanding.[1]

—JOHN WESLEY

Because I am a United Methodist pastor, it is natural that I turn for wisdom and guidance to the experience of John Wesley. I do this not only to seek insight into my question but also for a personal reason: I seek affirmation in United Methodism for a ministry rooted in contemplative prayer. (Although what follows may be an "in the United Methodist family" dialogue, I believe the issues I delve into have relevance for all Christians.)

Exploring the faith experience and writings of John Wesley yields three revelations pertinent to my question and call: First, John Wesley does offer an affirmation. Second, he also offers a caution and challenge. Third, Wesley formulates ways of doing what I sought to do: Awaken people to respond to God's longing for them and their longing for God.

John Wesley's journals—collected in Albert Outler's *John Wesley*—gave the affirmation I sought by disclosing the early years of his faith pilgrimage. I have divided Wesley's pilgrimage into stages, which describe the respective spiritual conditions of Wesley's experience.

The Holiness of Childhood

Wesley wrote the following:

> I believe, till I was about ten years old I had not sinned away that "washing of the Holy Ghost" [see Titus 3:5] which was given me in baptism, having been strictly educated and carefully taught that I could only be saved "by universal obedience, by keeping all the commandments of God," in the meaning of which I was diligently instructed.[2]

In other words, Wesley clung diligently to the statutes he was taught as a child: salvation by sinlessness. Until the age of ten, Wesley felt he was protected by the "washing" he received at his baptism.

Wandering from Things Holy

Childhood innocence gave way to youthful curiosity. Between the ages of ten and twenty-two, Wesley ceased to focus on religious faith. He still prayed, worshiped, and read scripture, but his faith during that period was nominal—not heartfelt. He wrote of his spiritual condition: "I had not all this while so much as a notion of inward holiness; nay, went on habitually and (for the most part) very contentedly, in some or other known sin."[3]

Awakening to God's Love

Wesley was not to remain in this superficial state. Through reading Thomas à Kempis's *Christian Pattern*, Wesley "began to see that true religion was seated in the heart, and that God's law extended to all our thoughts as well as words and actions."

Wesley then acquired a spiritual friend, something he had
never experienced before and which he found transforming: "I
began to alter the whole form of my conversation, and to set
in earnest upon 'a new life.' I set apart an hour or two a day for
religious retirement. I communicated every week. I watched
against all sin whether in word or deed. I began to aim at, and
pray for inward holiness."[4]

Clearly John Wesley's self-conscious faith pilgrimage had
begun. Continuing to comment on the period, he wrote,

> The light flowed in so mightily upon my soul that every-
> thing appeared in a new view. I cried to God for help and
> resolved not to prolong the time of obeying him as I had
> never done before. And by continued *endeavour to keep his
> whole law*, inward and outward, *to the utmost of my power*, I
> was persuaded that I should be accepted of him, and that I
> was even then in a state of salvation.[5]

In 1797 Wesley added this footnote: "And I believe I was."

Seeking Union with God through Deeds

As he suggested in his journal, Wesley endeavored to "keep
[God's] whole law": He visited prisons, assisted the poor, and
attended the sick. He began observing Wednesday and Friday
fasts. He strove against sin and followed other acts of self-denial.
He carefully "used…all the means of grace at all opportunities. I
omitted no occasion of doing good." He then wrote,

> All this I knew to be nothing, unless as it was directed
> toward inward holiness. Accordingly this, the image of God,
> was what I aimed at in all, by doing his will, not my own.
> Yet when, after continuing some years in this course, I
> apprehended myself to be near death, I could not find that
> all this gave me any comfort, or any assurance of acceptance
> with God.[6]

Wesley's dissatisfaction with the results of his outward obedience led to a predictable course of action.

Seeking Union with God through Introspection

Wesley swung to the other extreme at this stage in his life; he wrote, "Soon after, a contemplative man convinced me still more than I was convinced before, that outward works are nothing, being alone; and in several conversations instructed me how to pursue inward holiness, or union of the soul with God."[7]

Wesley followed this contemplative man's instructions with the same earnestness with which he obeyed God's words. These instructions included refraining from trust in outward works—Wesley ceased doing any at all—and learning the practice of mental prayer. Wesley termed this an exchange of salvation by outward works for salvation by inward works.

To his despair, Wesley still didn't obtain the relationship with God for which he hungered. This lifestyle also proved empty, and led him to the next phase of his pilgrimage.

Crisis

Wesley took a drastic action to console his spiritual hunger. He left his teaching position at Oxford to become a missionary to the Indians in the Colony of Georgia. He said later that he went not just to save the souls of the Indians but even more so, his own. While at sea the ship ran into "the skirts of a hurricane" so severe that its winds broke the main mast. Wesley was terrified, but to his amazement and shame a group of Moravians (German pietists who practiced rich spiritual disciplines) were not. They rode out the storm in calm demeanor, all the while singing hymns. Two things struck Wesley during that experience: First, trusting God in all circumstances, even life-threatening ones, was possible. Second, he had no such trust.

Wesley's stint in Georgia was a disaster, marked by significant failures in missions and in courtship. Consequently he returned to England in January 1738 in a state of spiritual darkness. The journey again proved treacherous; another storm threatened the lives of all passengers.

> In my return to England, January, 1738, being in imminent danger of death, and very uneasy on that account I was strongly convinced that the cause of that uneasiness was unbelief; and that the gaining of a true living faith was the "one thing needful" for me. But still I fixed not this faith on its right object: I meant only faith in God, not faith in or through Christ. Again, I knew not that I was wholly void of this faith; but, only thought, I had not enough of it.[8]

Wesley sought the counsel of a Moravian named Peter Böhler. Böhler challenged Wesley, not just about the degree of his faith but about its nature. Böhler exhorted Wesley to seek a "justifying, saving faith, a full reliance on the blood of Christ shed for *me*, a trust in Him, as *my* Christ, as my sole justification, sanctification, and redemption."[9]

The core of Wesley's crisis was his failure to realize that only God through Christ could fulfill his longing for God, which was awakened many years earlier when Wesley first began to seek God. Wesley clearly experienced the divine longing for him and his for God when he read Thomas à Kempis in 1725. His dilemma was attempting to satisfy his heart's longing first by deeds of charity and then by seeking inward insight. In this period of crisis his own life experience was teaching him that there was nothing he could do to calm the ache of his heart except trust that God in Jesus Christ was there to offer the union his heart so desperately sought. This he mysteriously was given at Aldersgate-Street on May 24, 1738.

Union with God through Christ

Wesley described this rich, illuminating moment in his life:

> In the evening I went very unwillingly to a society in Aldersgate-Street, where one was reading Luther's preface to the Epistle to the Romans. About a quarter before nine, while he was describing the change which God works in the heart through faith in Christ, I felt my heart strangely warmed. I felt I did trust in Christ, Christ alone for salvation: And an assurance was given me that he had taken away *my* sins, even *mine*, and saved *me* from the law of sin and death.
>
> I began to pray with all my might for those who had in a more especial manner despitefully used me and persecuted me. I then testified openly to all there, what I now first felt in my heart.[10]

It would be most inaccurate to say that after Aldersgate, Wesley enjoyed constant divine bliss. He was to know doubt, fear, and even faith crisis again. But Aldersgate did bring a crucial realization in John Wesley's faith journey: Only God's presence through Christ could satisfy his heart's desire for restored oneness with God. At Aldersgate, Wesley realized that God in Christ was giving him that for which his heart most ached. He was not required then to produce heroic acts of charity or illuminating inward insights. What was required of Wesley was belief that God in Christ was giving him his heart's desire. It was his for the trusting. That indeed is heartwarming, heart-restoring, and heart-reorienting.

With this view of Wesley's faith pilgrimage before us, let me share the way I feel affirmed in my call to contemplative prayer. It stems from the affinity I feel toward this spiritual father of my denomination. I strongly relate to Wesley's awakening moment through Thomas à Kempis in 1725. When I read Wesley's account of the moment he comprehended his longing: "I cried to God for help not to prolong the time of obeying him as I had never done before" and of his "continued endeavour to keep His whole law, inward and outward, to the utmost of my power,"[11] I recognize a familiar theme. Is this not a man who longs, as Biersdorf put it, "to attend to the presence of God—in community and in solitude, in action and reception, in pain and in happiness, in our doing and in our being"?

I too have tasted the rich goodness of God that Wesley describes and to which Biersdorf points. A close look at Wesley reveals the same ache living in his heart that lives in mine—the longing to tend to God in all my being and doing.

I also feel affinity with the depth of pain and struggle Wesley experienced from 1725 to 1738. Wesley honestly and openly records his fruitless efforts to respond to God's longing for him and his for God by developing outward and inward works of his own devising. His struggles with the terror of facing death echo Thomas Merton's description of the dread one encounters in contemplative prayer. Wesley recorded that being in danger of death caused him great horror. In his book *Contemplative Prayer*, Merton wrote of similar feelings:

> The monk confronts his own humanity and that of his world at the deepest and most central point where the void seems to open out into black despair. The monk confronts this serious possibility, and rejects it.... The option of absolute despair is turned into perfect hope by the pure and humble supplication of monastic prayer. The monk faces the worst, and discovers in it the hope of the best. From the darkness comes the light. From death, life. From the abyss there comes, unaccountably, the mysterious gift of the new, to transform the created and redeemed world, and to re-establish all things in Christ.[12]

The call to contemplative prayer, as I have experienced it and as Merton describes it, includes being drawn into a wilderness of emptiness and despair. The cause for despair is the realization of helplessness: There is nothing one or anyone else can do to dispel this dark void of the heart. The good news that leads a contemplative to prayer, not suicide, is the deep revelation of faith that is the gospel. This revelation comes as a trustful knowing in the heart that the crucified and risen Jesus is present in this wilderness. It is the realization that the new life of Christ is to be found in this place where death seemingly reigns. In Christ the heart's place of utter despair becomes the place of abiding faith, hope, and love.

This struggle of faith comes to all of us. I believe it came to Wesley in the years 1725–38. I believe at Aldersgate he found the assurance that neither outer nor inner works could afford— a strangely warming realization that God's love in Christ was more powerful than the forces of death and despair. Wesley received the assurance that through faith in Christ abiding, all-powerful love was alive in him forever!

I feel affinity with the depth of Wesley's struggle. I am beginning to feel affinity with the assurance of faith Wesley experienced at Aldersgate. One final way I relate to John Wesley is in the countless number of times he speaks of "religion of the heart." Here are but two of a multitude of samples that appear in Wesley's sermons and journal:

> That "circumcision is that of the heart, in the spirit, and not in the letter,"—that distinguishing mark of a true follower of Christ, of one who is in a state of acceptance with God, is not either outward circumcision, or baptism, or any other outward form, but a right state of soul, a mind and spirit renewed after the image of Him that created it.[13]

> But in the process of time, when the "love of many waxed cold," some began to mistake the *means* for the *end* and to place religion rather in doing those outward works, than in a heart renewed after the image of God.[14]

Wesley aptly described his heart's longing to live in the presence of God. He professed that one finds satisfaction of this longing in a faith that God's Christ gives us what we seek. These truths underlie a contemplative call to ministry and this book's question. I find affirmation for both in my denomination's spiritual father.

Wesley's Caution and Challenge

Despite the parallels I've identified between Wesley's spiritual journey and the call of the contemplative, Wesley himself was suspicious for a time of "things contemplative." The teachings of a contemplative movement called Quietism, which recommended the same inward devotion as the sole means to salvation, disturbed him. Quietism eventually grew influential enough to become a threat to the Methodist movement. Wesley addressed this threat in his sermon "Upon Our Lord's Sermon on the Mount I."

I began this chapter with Wesley's opening words in that sermon. In the first two paragraphs Wesley stressed the beauty and the importance of heeding "the inward [one] of the heart" and nurturing that growth. He then proceeded to lay out his opponent's position that speaks of religion only as an inward venture at the expense of outward sharing and deeds of love.

> If religion, therefore, were carried no farther than this, they could have no doubt concerning it; they should have no objection against pursuing it with the whole ardor of their souls. "But why," say they, "is it clogged with other things? What need of loading it with *doing* and *suffering*? These are

what damp the vigour of the soul, and sinks it down to
earth again. Is it not enough to "follow after charity"; to
soar upon the wings of love? Will it not suffice to worship
God, who is a Spirit, with the spirit of our minds, without
encumbering ourselves with outward things, or even thinking of them at all? Is it better that the whole extent of our
thought be taken up with high and heavenly contemplation?[15]

Wesley responded to this list of seductive questions with a
resounding No! His text was, "You are the salt of the
earth.... You are the light of the world. A city built on a hill
cannot be hid" (Matt. 5:13-14). The thrust of Wesley's message
was that the light, which we have come to know in the sanctuary of our hearts, is given to us to be seen by and shared
with others. Reducing Christianity to a quiet, solitary gazing
at our inner light is to destroy its very fabric. Wesley said
Christianity is "essentially a social religion"—we know this
light in communion with fellow believers. We are called to
share this light in order that others will know God's love.

Wesley suggests a well-formulated caution to anyone
called to contemplation. I believe he knew well its seductive
dangers because he knew what the heart of a true contemplative was. I believe he had one.

It is interesting to note how Wesley's attacks on an inwardness gone astray parallel modern-day contemplative Thomas
Merton's remarks on what he termed the illusion of "the individualist." Merton wrote,

The interior life of the individualist is precisely the kind of
life that closes in on itself without dread, and rests in itself
with more or less permanent satisfaction. It is to some
extent immune to dread, and is able to take the inevitable

constrictions and lesions of an inner life complacently enough,…Individualism in prayer is content, precisely with the petty consolations of devotionalism and sentimentality.

Wesley with his confrontation of the "Quietists" and Merton with his confrontation of the "individualist" refer to a spirituality rooted in self-contemplation rather than a contemplation rooted in divine mercy, illumination, and acts of love. One called by God to contemplative prayer needs to hear the caution both men raise about a self-centered spirituality: A thinly veiled narcissism is a spirituality that avoids God, others, and one's true self.

In his later years, however, Wesley acknowledged that contemplation need not lead to spiritual narcissism. He wrote of meeting "mystics" who through contemplation were connected with God, others, and self. E. H. Sugden, Wesley biographer, wrote, "In his cooler moments he was quite ready to appreciate the better elements of Mysticism, and to admit that its earlier exponents were men of love experimentally acquainted with true inward religion; burning and shining lights, and such as had well deserved of the Church of Christ."[17]

Merton and Wesley are brothers who share God's love as they have come to know and long for this love in Jesus Christ. Both men teach us to be suspect of a peace of the heart that rests complacent and indifferent toward human suffering; of an inwardness that isolates one from relating to others; and of "an interest in God" that does not lead to sharing with others the love God has given.

Wesley and Awakening the Divine Longing

Wesley preached a sermon entitled "The Means of Grace," in which he spoke of ways God in Christ awakens us. These are embodied in five "means of grace" that Christ ordained and exemplified in his life and teachings: prayer, searching the scriptures, the Lord's Supper, fasting, and Christian community. It is important, Wesley said, not to confuse the means of grace with the Source of grace. Prayer should not be seen as an end itself nor should scripture or the Lord's Supper. Each is instead a means, or a window, into God's love for us that in turn awakens our love for God. Wesley also recommended discernment about which means to employ, when, and with whom.

Prayer

To John Wesley prayer was the "breath of the spiritual life . . . the grand means of drawing near to God." His own prayer pattern is interesting and instructive. He began each day in private prayer, believing that one waited in quietness to receive the blessing of God. He developed a weekly pattern that consisted of waiting for God in quietness, written prayers from a variety of sources, plus time for spontaneous prayers. He focused on one topic a day.

But Wesley also trained his mind to pray hourly. This was an inward practice that consisted of brief sentence prayers of praise followed by five to seven minutes in meditation. According to Wesley scholar Steve Harper, Wesley, while praying sentence prayers did not stop what he was doing: "Wesley had trained himself to turn his 'inner voice' to the Creator."[18] Wesley's discipline reminds me of the classic Jesus Prayer we're instructed to integrate with our breathing—he seemed to understand it at a practical level.

Wesley also concluded his day with a time of prayer. He followed his morning pattern but added a review of the day with appropriate confession for sins committed. In this way he prepared his heart to rest in God as he slept.

Wesley's sources of prayers were *The Book of Common Prayer*, prayers written by others, and of course the spontaneous, deep movement of God's Spirit in his heart. He prayed aloud and silently, and he incorporated his prayers with hymn singing and scripture.

Finally Wesley placed a great deal of importance on praying with others. This, of course, took the form of corporate worship in the Anglican church and regular small-group prayer times. Clearly Wesley emphasized prayer as a means of connecting with the divine longing.

Scripture

For Wesley scripture was the objective base for one's spiritual life as well as the corporate life of the church. Scripture was not a cold, objective standard; Wesley felt its primary value was its unique ability to bring men and women into an encounter with God. In a similar light, Hazelyn McComas, a friend and Bible teacher, taught me to see scripture as the meeting place between God and human beings, a very Wesleyan view. For Wesley, scripture was devotional, not legalistic.

Wesley's reading of scripture was systematic, following the daily readings in *The Book of Common Prayer*. His intent was not accomplishing a given quantity but encountering God. Wesley allowed himself to be drawn to the verse or verses that seemed to address him, and there he would linger. Wesley recommended reading in an unhurried, reverent manner. He wrote, "Here then I am, far from the busy ways of [the world]. I sit down alone: Only God is here. In his presence I open, I read his book, for this end, to find the way to heaven."[19]

Wesley also valued scholarly background as a source to aid him and other readers to understand God's truth. Wesley believed that when viewed in a comprehensive way, the Bible could speak to every aspect of our lives. Wesley's own method of scripture reading contained these elements:

• Dailyness—morning and evening;
• Singleness of purpose—to know God's will;
• Correlation—to compare scripture with scripture;
• Prayerfulness—to receive the instruction of the Holy Spirit;
• Resolution—to put into practice what is learned.[20]

That last point was crucial. Wesley wrote, "Whatever light you receive should be used to the uttermost, and that immediately." In other words, the truth of God revealed in scripture was to be lived in people's lives and shared with others. People were to examine their attitudes, feelings, and actions in the light of scripture and then act in the light of their encounter.

Wesley also stressed that what we learn in scripture we are called by God to teach to others—in sensitive and loving ways, never being dogmatic or pushy. And Wesley saw that scripture was to be experienced corporately. This meant regular exposure to God's Word in worship and prayerful study in various small-group settings.

The Lord's Supper

Albert Outler, in his introduction to a Wesley sermon on Holy Communion, wrote, "The Wesleys conceived of sacramental grace as God's love in action in the lives of faithful men [and women] at worship. The Lord's Supper is the paradigm of all 'the means of grace'—the chief actual means of actual grace and, as such, literally indispensable in the Christian life."[21]

Wesley saw the sacrament of the Lord's Supper first as a memorial meal. It was a time for Christians to recall in a fresh way the event of Christ's redemptive act. Second, it was the real presence of Christ: By his own choice the risen Christ was truly present, through the Holy Spirit, when the sacrament was observed. Third, the Lord's Supper served as a pledge. It was a promise of future glory that awaits Christians in heaven. The sacrament acts as an assurance of the final outcome of our faith.

Steve Harper points out that these three dimensions contain the elements of contemplation, experience, and hope. Wesley's own words are these: "Let every one, therefore, who has either any desire to please God, or any love of his [or her] own soul, obey God, and consult the good of his [or her] own soul, by communicating every time he [or she] can."[22]

Wesley had thoughts on the way we should approach Communion. We are to do it frequently: "No [one] can have any pretense to Christian piety, who does not receive it (not once a month, but) as often as he [or she] can." Qualifying to receive the sacrament did not depend on the character of the recipient; it depended upon a candidate's preparation of herself or himself. Had the recipient examined his or her heart? Was he or she humble and penitent of spirit, searching for and trusting in the divine mercy of this holy meal?

Fasting

Wesley noted three types of fasting: eating no food at all; abstinence from certain foods (to be used when for health reasons one could not fast entirely); and abstaining from pleasant foods, which Wesley called "the lowest kind of fasting."

From 1725 to 1738 Wesley fasted two days a week, Wednesday and Friday. After 1738 he reduced this to Friday only. The most common practice was to refrain from eating from morning until evening. Wesley cautioned against turning this discipline into some kind of mortification of the body; to him its main value lay in setting mealtime aside for prayer. Its purpose was that it be done unto the Lord, with our eye singly fixed on him.

Let our intention herein be this, and this alone, to glorify our Father which is in heaven; to express our sorrow and shame for our manifold transgressions of His holy law; to wait for an increase of purifying grace, drawing our affections to things above; to add seriousness and earnestness to our prayers; to avert the wrath of God, and to attain all the great and precious promises which He hath made to us in Jesus Christ.[23]

Christian Conferences

There were two keys to the success of the early Methodist movement: revival meetings that featured Charles Wesley's hymns and John Wesley's preaching, and the formation of converts into Christian Societies. (Today we would call them covenant groups.) These societies had three organizational levels.

First was the overarching society that consisted of up to 250 people. These were broken into classes of up to twelve people. One did not have to be a committed Christian to belong either to the Society or a class; one did, however, have to express and demonstrate a serious desire to seek God. Bands, same-sex small groups no larger than ten persons, made up the third level, and they were for only committed believers. The rationale was a wise one. With committed believers there was a capacity for vulnerability that may or may not be present in one who is still searching for God.

Wesley strongly emphasized Christian Conferences as a key means of grace. After visiting a site in which the society structure had broken down, Wesley wrote, "I was more convinced than ever, that the preaching like an Apostle, without joining together those that are awakened, and training them up in the ways of God, is only begetting children for the murderer."[24]

The classes and bands met weekly. They were the arena that rekindled the candle of faith, where people met for renewal and transformation of their lives into Christ's image, where money was raised to support the poor and the work of Methodist preachers, and where people faced the call to reach out and share the grace they were receiving. In short, the Society was a place to awaken and feed one's longing for God.

Wesley would be the last to limit God's awakening grace to these five means. He wrote, "Are there no other means than these, whereby God is pleased, frequently, yea, ordinarily, to convey his grace to them that either love or fear him? Surely there are works of mercy, as well as works of piety, which are real means of grace." These other means Wesley termed "prudential means of grace," or principles for living the life of holiness to which Christ calls believers: doing no harm, doing good, and attending upon all ordinances of God. These became the Rules of the Methodist Society.

Of the first, "do no harm," Harper wrote, "Wesley's prohibitions were not binders so much as they were boundaries. He knew that antinomianism resulted in spiritual inertia and moral chaos."[24] In essence this category was a delineation of what a believer needed to say "no" to in order to grow in holiness. Gossiping, overeating, and overblown materialistic appetites fell in this category.

"Doing good" meant actively benefiting the physical welfare of others. This included the provision of food, clothing, and shelter, and visiting the sick and prisoners. It also meant benefiting the souls of others through evangelism and discipleship.

"Attending upon the ordinances of God" linked these social principles with the spiritual means of grace through which one continued to know God's love and desire that love. One can see how integrated and holistic was John Wesley's way of awakening and forming Christians and Christian community.

Conclusion

Reading Wesley confirms that a pastoral ministry rooted in contemplative prayer has its place in my particular tradition. John Wesley was aware of and struggled with his heart's longing for God. Wesley came to know that only faith in Christ Jesus could satisfy this longing. It is a longing only God can give and only God can satisfy, and that in the cross of Jesus Christ. Once he understood this, faith in Christ's guiding presence led Wesley to a life of living and sharing this love.

Wesley has led me anew to the foundation of faith in Christ as the cornerstone for offering a ministry rooted in contemplative prayer. With piercing gaze he asks, "Does your contemplative prayer connect you in Christ with others? Do you find in your prayer time the desire to make the call on the widows of the congregation, the desire to listen deeply for the movement of the hidden Christ in the words, thoughts, and feelings of my people as you meet them in counseling, in committee meetings, and in shared ministries? Does your prayer time create in you a joy to praise and share God's Word in worship and daily living? "Beware," he continues, "of prayer that does not stir such a desire. Be fervent in prayer that does."

Wesley offers practical guidance on ways to awaken people to God's longing for them and their longing for God. When used with prayerful discernment Wesley's instituted means of grace are as applicable and needed today as they were in his time. Wesley challenges me to create the equivalent of his ministry.

THE LONGING IN CONTEMPORARY WRITINGS

Whenever one seems to get lost and confused it is often due to losing touch with this childlike yearning for union with God.[1]

—JAMES FINLEY

Macrina Wiederkehr described it earlier: the divine longing in my heart and the hearts of others as a "silent cry that yearns for understanding." I explore this "silent cry" by turning to the thoughts of contemporary spiritual writers. I bring these questions: *What does God require of us to understand the divine longing? What is the nature of the divine longing? What is the nature of the pastoral role and task to awaken people to the divine longing? What are the ways spiritual leaders can awaken people to respond to the divine longing?*

The answers I found penetrated my understanding on a deep level. Through such respected writers as Rueben Job, Kathleen Norris, James Finley, Thomas Merton, and the ancient but contemporary voice of the Apostle Paul, I discovered in a profoundly personal way the ways we can tap and be tapped by the longing.

What Does God Require of Me?

Several years ago I ran across an unpublished paper given by
Rueben Job, retired United Methodist bishop, to a group of
Dakota United Methodist clergy entitled "The Cost of
Spirituality."² Job framed his paper around "five windows" into
the cost of spirituality. As I read the paper I felt Rueben Job
was offering me five windows into the divine longing. As Job's
words led me to look through each of these windows, I found
myself coming to realize more fully what God was requiring
of me to understand the divine longing.

I will convey what I experienced and learned in the form
of an imaginary tour into the inner mansion of my heart. The
tour reveals important truths that the divine longing asks me
to know and embrace.

Every tour begins with some impetus. This one begins
with an invitation from Rueben Job: "Seek with me to cut
through the mist of culture and excuse to the very center of
the issue of spirituality—what does it mean for us to walk
with God today?"

I think about Job's question. To walk with God isn't to
study or even to explore God's nature. It is to accompany. It is
to be with and do for. This life-and-death question determines
my basic perception and life direction.

Job begins by telling me what entering this house, or
embracing the divine longing, will not accomplish: the
appointment of my dreams, success and well-being for my children, support for my marriage, material security, or escape from
illness or tragedy. Job reminds me that my coming to God's
temple with such desires only belies how far I am from the rad-
ical obedience Jesus requires. "Enter this place and prepare to
become a suffering servant, not a superstar," he says.

I stand on the porch of my inner mansion, realizing that this place isn't what I hoped for. My self-created spiritual "wisdom" is about to be showed for the sham it is. But Job's presence and question stir in me a hunger for the spiritual wisdom of God. I decide to follow him to the first window. As I draw near the light that streams from it, I see a word above it: *Faith*.

Window 1: Faith

Job begins, "Is there any among us"—Us! I suddenly realize that though I have entered the deepest part of me, this part of me is connected with a company of others. The company includes my family, friends, and colleagues; literary and historic figures dead and alive; the Dakota pastors who first heard Job's talk; and people from my congregation. As I continue to listen, though I appear to be alone, I am actually with a host of believers.

Job asks me and the unseen pilgrims, *Is there anyone who has not known a dryness of the spirit that strangles prayer?* anyone who has at least not come close to a dark night of the soul? Been alone? forsaken? had times of no assurance of the Divine Presence? Which one of us hasn't approached ministry certain it was all up to us? Which one of us has not capitulated to the faithlessness of our culture?

I listen and feel known and comforted. But the soft empathy in Job's eyes turns intense. He turns from one who comforts to one who also challenges: "It is possible to believe again, to live out our lives on the basis of the call and will of God. There is a paradox here. Faith is a gift from God. However, we must not only be open to receive the gift of faith, we must practice it, live by it, order our lives by it. Bonhoeffer reflected this paradox: 'Only those who obey can believe and only those who believe can obey.'"

Job's next words really hit home: "We often do not have faith because we do not obey what we already know." Standing in the temple of my own divine longing, I start to recognize the countless times I have turned from what my heart knows is true and has longed to tell me. "Why? Why? Why?" pours out of me not as a question but as an acknowledgement of my own self-betrayal. Job continues, "Authentic spirituality requires us to ask, Lord, what do you want me to be, to become, to do?"

Job's words remind me of what I have known to be true. I cannot make the divine longing God has given me into what I want it to be: a purveyor of gifts like those Job listed earlier. I can only let this divine gift make me into what it wants me to "be, become, do." Standing before the light of this window marked *Faith* I realize that understanding the deep desire of my heart depends upon my commitment to trust that God's desire is in me and to obey this divine desire, this gift of grace.

Standing in the much-appreciated light of the window of Faith, I feel a desire to follow Job to the next window.

Window 2: Single-mindedness

Job turns to the teachings of Jesus and reads, "You shall love the Lord your God with all your heart, and with all your soul, and with all your mind" (Matt. 22:37) and "Strive first for the kingdom of God and his righteousness, and all these things will be given to you as well" (Matt. 6:33).

Job interprets, "The call to the Kingdom was a call to forsake everything. . . . No divided loyalties, no half hearted commitments, no series of priorities. [These passages reveal] just one simple demand that was uttered and underscored again and again. Søren Kierkegaard said, 'To will one thing is to know God.'"

The longing is not one I can place alongside other desires of my heart, those that fill my mind and so often capture my attention. In this temple of divine longing I see these pressing desires, ambitions, and feelings in a new way. To enter this temple I need to let these other desires be silenced and open myself to the light that lives in the secret, sacred center of my being. I cringe and withdraw as I think, *I want to will one thing, but I don't.* I run after many things, constantly forgetting this deepest desire. But my knowing guide addresses this fact of my life as well:

> For whatever reasons, we have not placed God first, it is hard to do—many have started there but do not now practice or reflect that singlemindedness of which Jesus and the saints spoke so often. But, our present place in our journey is unimportant. What is important is our awareness of the call to singleminded attention to God.

I move closer to this window's light. I remember Peter's denial and Paul's "I can will what is right, but I cannot do it" (Rom. 7:18). I remember that failure is permitted but faithlessness is not.

Job helps me see that singleminded knowing of the divine longing is not a constant state of understanding. It is a decision to trust always that the divine longing is around me and in me, waiting to be revealed when I trust and obey.

As I, and the others I sense to be with me, move deeper within the temple of divine longing, my heart feels a deep peace. I and the others are more silent and open as we come to the third window. This window is a bit larger and more expansive than the rest—or is my perception becoming broader? Above this window my fellow pilgrims and I see the word *Solidarity.*

Window 3: Solidarity

Job addresses the nature of the peace and expansiveness we feel:

> Authentic spirituality that is rooted in God is costly spiri-
> tuality because it identifies with neighbor. There is only
> one human family and every person is a part of that fami-
> ly. Thus the weakness, ignorance, oppression, agony, suffer-
> ing, and brokenness of all is a part of the pain that the
> Spirit-led and Spirit-filled person takes up as both tragedy
> and triumph of being a child of God.

Job adds, of course, that there is a peace and freedom from fear
and guilt that comes to one who walks with God. They come
as gifts; they are not the aim. They are not wages earned at the
expense of others. Because my heart has known so much fear,
shame, and guilt, I constantly turn my heart's desire for God
into a desire for peace and a release from these choking feelings. As I stand in the light of this window, I begin to feel how
narrow and isolating this "cheap" spiritual desire is. This light
also reveals that every person I see has the same wounds of the
heart. It feels healing to focus upon the light and not on my
wounds, to focus upon the light touching my and others'
wounds. Standing before the window called Solidarity, I realize
God's longing is to heal these wounds that break the human
heart and bind it in sin. The light coming from this window
joins us, the wounded of the earth, together in community.

Job comments on how colorless and tame the church has
become in its turning from the hurts that cripple our world.
He concludes his remarks at this window: "I do not know
where God is calling us. But I do know [God] calls us to stop
pretending, to get out of the cave and really begin to live the
life of faith we often profess."

Job indicates there is more to be seen.

Window 4: Self-denial

I find myself nodding in affirmation as Job confronts what has become an idol of the church—a focus upon development of self:

> We have much to learn from the social sciences about human behavior and development. Unfortunately, we have often allowed these sciences to become our theology rather than [to] inform our theology. We have placed self, human development, and our personal desire at the center of the universe. There can be only one center of the universe and that center is God. . . . A great barrier to spiritual growth is self-centeredness, for spirituality [and our heart's longing for God] is God centeredness. If we are even to begin this journey, we must leave self behind.

Job turns to New Testament passages that call for disciples of Christ to deny self: Romans 1:1— "Paul, a servant of Jesus Christ"; James 1:1— "James, a servant of God and of the Lord Jesus Christ"; Galatians 5:13—"Through love become slaves to one another." He then quotes Jesus, "If any want to become my followers, let them deny themselves and take up their cross and follow me" (Matt. 16:24).

I trust Rueben Job. I trust the New Testament writers. I obviously trust Jesus. Job has been right to lead me to this window. Christian writers down through the ages have taught that self-denial is one of the costs of spiritual growth, the cost of knowing and living in the house of divine longing.

But I find an authentic embracing of this window's light blocked by a perception of self-denial that is in fact masked self-hate. I actually discovered this over a month's time. Illumination came through recalling an experience I had the day after Easter a couple of years ago. I was on retreat, far enough removed from the stresses of Easter to catch a glimpse of the hidden agenda I had brought to my worship leadership Easter morning. We can call the following a "waking dream."

> I am standing in the chancel of the church. The church altar has been replaced by the mouth of the empty tomb of Jesus' resurrection. However, I am not wanting the people to see the empty tomb. What I really want is the people to see me standing in front of the empty tomb. I want praise and adulation to be directed to me, not the risen Lord Jesus. I clearly do not want to share any of this chancel-turned-stage with the one who rose from the tomb.

I felt bemused, troubled, and blessed by this post-Easter meditation. The disturbing part is the self-promotion evidently bubbling beneath my surface. The blessing is that I have been given to see a me who has no interest in God's love. This me is not only incapable of bringing Christ's love to others; it attempts to strangle that love in myself. It is in fact a fear to be who I am before God and others. This neurotic loathing does not equip me to follow Christ. It creates a passivity and compliance that does not witness to God's love. I cannot and do not believe that this is the kind of self-denial Job is counseling. And now that I recognize it, I can deal with it.

I believe that what I met in my Easter meditation is what Paul in Colossians calls "the old self." "Do not lie to one another, seeing that you have stripped off the old self with its practices and have clothed yourselves with the new self, which is being renewed in knowledge according to the image of its creator" (Col. 3:9-10). James Finley quotes Thomas Merton's view of original sin: "To say I was born in sin is to say I came into the world with a false self."[3] The "false self" is the part of us that has come into existence by choosing to believe the snake's lie and is still under that lie's evil spell. Finley writes, "There is something in me that puts on fig leaves of concealment, kills my brother [and sister], builds towers of confusion, and brings cosmic chaos upon the earth. There is something in me that loves darkness rather than light, that rejects God and thereby rejects my own deepest reality as a human person made in the image and likeness of God."[4]

Paul's "old self" or Merton's "false self" is the opponent in us that we must face, confess, and crucify in Christ. I believe this is the self that Jesus, the New Testament writers, and Rueben Job call us to deny. If I do not take the time to confront this self in me that alienates me from God's longing for me and my longing for God, and say with heartfelt clarity, "This is not who I am or who I want to be," I shall remain blind to the true nature of the divine longing and caught forever in an all-pervading web of self-deception.

I agree fully with Job's words as we leave this window: "When we are ready to confess our rebellion against God, deny ourselves and place God at the center of life, then we will be ready to grow spiritually."[5]

Window 5: Vulnerability

Job's comments convey the importance of this window:

> Vulnerability is related to all the other windows and may even be the shutters on them all. All of us are of course vulnerable. We are all weak. We all make mistakes. We will all die. We all have one point that if touched will bring us down. But do we ever admit it? Never! Our barrier to spirituality and to community is our desire, no, our sin of pretending to be invulnerable, pretending to be God.

He echoes Finley's insights about the false self, saying, "As we place the false fronts out there to protect ourselves and to hide from one another we also hide from God. And soon we have become hidden even from ourselves, and we no longer know who we are and what we are called to become."

As he has done so often through this tour of the cost of Christian spirituality, Job turns our attention to Jesus. Now the Jesus of which he speaks is not the strong one who silenced the Pharisees with a wise word and healed afflicted people with a gentle touch; the Jesus he speaks of now entered the dark silence of the cross and himself was afflicted in body and spirit. He now speaks of the Jesus emptied of "power, the rightful place, the majesty . . . the glory." He speaks of the Jesus who became a suffering servant, a dying servant. Jesus is our model of vulnerability.

Job speaks about "the miracle" we find in this vulnerability.

The miracle is that at the moment vulnerability is born, God's power is released. Not to protect from pain or crucifixion. But power to live, power to reconcile, power to hang on, power to forgive, power to heal, power to witness, and power to make whole. . . . We will not grow spiritually until we become vulnerable. To become vulnerable and defenseless is to open the windows of heaven and release the power of the Spirit.

The window's light unearths my confessional litany of "despites":

Despite having read and embraced Henri Nouwen's *The Wounded Healer* as both permission and stance to offer ministry;

Despite having completed of a doctor of ministry degree that has emphasized and modeled vulnerability as the way to know God and offer ministry;

Despite having experienced in numerous doctor of ministry seminars the gift of healing that comes when others and I have chosen to be vulnerable;

Despite preaching, teaching, and counseling vulnerability as the doorway to Christian growth—I do not come to Window 5 willingly. In fact, without divine guidance through a wise leader such as Rueben Job, I do not know how to find my way to this window, "the shutters" to all the other windows of the mansion of my divine longing.

I find it important to name the reason for my unwillingness and blindness, which is a deeply rooted frailty of the heart. James Finley writes in *The Awakening Call,* "Subject to sin, our hearts are shot through with frailty."[5] Subject to sin, I daily repeat the story of the Fall. After all these years of ministry, I know I belong to God. I know my heart longs for intimacy with God. Yet like Adam and Eve after the Fall, I flee from God's presence. This ancient story names my fear and my shame: It is my nakedness. Job is exactly right. I fear accepting and disclosing the fact that I am vulnerable. I stand in the light of this window and see how everything I do in life is shadowed by a desire to make myself invulnerable. (That includes, of course, writing a book on the divine longing.)

This window reminds me that my understanding the nature of the divine longing is contingent upon my becoming vulnerable. But how do I become what in fact I dread becoming? Job points me to Jesus, who chose vulnerability, chose to be empty, chose to be naked. In doing so he revealed the miracle of God's love and power that lives in the vulnerable, empty, naked place of the human heart…of my heart.

By leading me to this pivotal window called Vulnerability, Job has showed me anew that my understanding the nature of the divine longing rests not on insight or heroic act but in my believing in this miracle. The word of Christ's mercy and healing, not the word of condemnation, lives among the frail, bro-

ken pieces of my heart. Job invites me to trust that the nature
of the divine longing is to be found in the place within where
my heart knows a deep, vulnerable hunger.

Standing in this window's light, I turn to the fragility of
my heart. I meet a loneliness that seems vast. I walk into this
loneliness and feel an empty silence. There I know a poverty of
spirit that is a permanent fixture in my heart. Knowing how
permanent it is, I feel a sense of futility that tempts me to
despair about who I am and about life in general. But I do
not! Here in this place of my vulnerability and permanent
incompleteness, I feel I am being met. I feel I am being
accompanied by a Presence. This Presence knows me and gen-
tly smiles at the futility and silliness of what I have wanted to
do with my life.

But this is not a smile of indulgence. I sense the Presence
is not amused about the ways I have chosen to run away and
waste the gift of my life. This Presence has met me in this des-
olate place to judge my desire to have life on my terms and to
seek an invulnerability that is not of my nature. And in this
judgment, I am realizing that the peace I have sought is to be
found in a desire that seems most true to my nature: the desire
to love always this Presence that gives me miraculous love in
the fragile, vulnerable place of my being. Here at this fifth
window I awaken and respond to God's longing for me and
my lost and restored longing for God.

As I near this tour's end, I realize I have been walking in a
deepening spiral in the mansion of my divine longing. The
window of Vulnerability has brought me back to the window
of Faith. And I also see in a clearer way what understanding
the divine longing requires of me: Faith, Single-mindedness,
Solidarity, Self-denial, and Vulnerability. Through these win-

dows comes the light that reveals the divine longing of my heart.

What Is the Nature of the Divine Longing?

Just as Job had windows into the cost of spirituality, I wish to offer glimpses into the nature of the divine longing, for "glimpses" are all we are given to know about this core truth of our hearts. The first glimpse is the report of a person's experiencing this divine longing. The second is a theological reflection on its nature. The third gives several metaphors that illuminate the meaning of the term *divine longing*.

Glimpse 1: Experience

James Finley gives this rich recounting in *The Awakening Call* of one (presumably himself) who visits the hospital room of his dying father:

> So you rush to the hospital, countless questions and concerns hold you in their grasp. And when you arrive it is as terrible as you imagined. But what you never expected is also true. He says something wise yet childlike. In his hands, clasped upon your own, you become your father's father or mother. And as this child that conceived you slips away over the edge of some great, unseen secret, a vastness opens within you. You walk away silenced and for a moment, wise, in the humbling realization that we live our lives seeing only the tip of the iceberg. And all that does appear above the surface does so only fleetingly as a brief manifestation of some unseen abyss that endows the smallest of things and events with a value beyond comprehension.[6]

Finley's story contains key characteristics of the divine longing. It is "some great, unseen secret [that] opens within you."

His metaphorical language reveals God's longing for us as "some unseen abyss that endows the smallest of things and events with a value beyond comprehension." If his words stir in you as they do in me an awareness of an unseen secret you have caught and been caught by an understanding of God's longing for you and your longing for God.

Glimpse 2: Reflection

Theological reflection upon this aspect of the human heart can prove risky, for theological abstractions can bury the very reality we seek to understand. But the following reflection from Thomas Merton's *Contemplative Prayer* lends important theological and psychological clarity while being faithful to the reality described: "The concept of 'the heart' might well be analyzed here. It refers to the deepest psychological ground of one's personality, the inner sanctuary where self-awareness goes beyond analytical reflection and opens out into meta-physical and theological confrontation with the Abyss of the unknown yet present—one who is more intimate to us than we are to ourselves."[7]

This reflection is packed with insight about the divine longing of the heart. It tells us that our longing is at the core of who we are—it defines our identity. Our longing is holy in nature. And, though part of us, it is beyond us and incompre-hensible to our rational mind. Finally, this part of us yields an intimacy with God in which we feel close to God and our-selves.

Glimpse 3: Metaphor

Finley has taught me that to attempt to offer a definition of the divine longing would be like passing out an X-ray of your mother's chest as a picture of her. To understand, we need metaphors. Finley's book *The Awakening Call* offers several: "silent music," "the wind [within] that blows where it wills," "the inmost Self," "the holy desire" (from Saint Augustine), and "the little secret love" (from *The Cloud of Unknowing*). To Finley's list I would add Macrina Wiederkehr's "silent cry seeking understanding."

These last two in particular point us to the obscure nature of this longing. In fact the word *obscure* appears quite often in both Thomas Merton's *Contemplative Prayer* and Finley's *The Awakening Call*. *Obscure* here does not mean confusing or obtuse but rather "not immediately apparent to us." The longing is with us, yet easy to overlook.

Finley offers two reasons why we experience the divine longing in such an elusive manner. First is our sin; we are drawn from experiencing this life-giving desire by our choosing other desires in life. We are unfaithful to our heart's deep hunger. We whore after other loves and lose touch with God and our heart's true love.

Second is our need to control. This desire is a gift from God that is never ours to possess or command—"The wind blows where it chooses" (John 3:8). Sometimes the elusive nature of the gift teaches us humility and reminds us who is the Source of this desire. The gift side of the "obscurity" fosters a prayerful dependence upon God.

Before leaving this list of metaphors, I want to add one final understanding. As we see the divine longing as a "little secret love," "little" reminds us that it is not ostentatious by nature. "Secret" reminds us that our longing for God and God's longing for us are a deep mystery that we carry and that mysteriously carries us. "Love" reminds us that this longing is not an introspective truth we know in the privacy of our hearts. It is our desire to be present to God's love and to serve others in the spirit of God's love.

What Is the Nature of the Pastoral Role?

This question is an important one, for it defines our ministry. And for a good period of time, it was a question whose answer proved elusive to me. I did not grasp the nature of this ministry because I understood my ministry primarily as a function one performs rather than a relationship one offers. By "function" I mean seeing the pastor primarily as a resource for creative ideas, theological knowledge, scriptural understanding, pastoral insights, and practical programming methods to serve the church and its people. I do not want to diminish the importance of any of these in offering ministry. But I have come to see that there is more to a minister, particularly one whose intention is to see and awaken in others the divine longing. Ministry as relationship grows from something the heart is given to see and offer. Hence I have learned that we are looking for a metaphor that names and gives glimpses into a relationship that one offers, not a definition or description of something one performs.

Kathleen Norris's recounting of the impact that a Benedictine community had on her gave me the name for and the underlying understanding of this kind of ministry. She wrote that it was the "hospitality" afforded to her that awakened her to God's love for her and her love for God. I believe the term *hospitality* points us to the nature of this ministry and the ministerial role one needs to assume. In her book *Dakota*, Norris wrote that the hospitality she experienced was marked by "an open response to the dignity of each and every person."[8] It is receiving the stranger on his or her terms. And this hospitality is anchored in and flows from the holy silence that lives in the center of a monk's heart.

The holy silence of the heart is the source for this kind of hospitality, a hospitality that makes room for the stranger—who really is all of us in our quest for God. Finding this hospitality is finding our true destiny. Norris wrote, "[This hospitality] does not lead aside or astray, but home. It won't necessarily make you a follower or even a fan of monks; instead, it will encourage you to examine and define your own deepest commitments." Later she added that the hospitality helped "me to become who I wanted to be as a writer, as a wife, even as a Presbyterian, and that this was as it should be."[9]

As I reflected upon what Kathleen Norris had written about the ministry of Benedictine hospitality, I realized how much her account paralleled my experience with contemplative prayer. My awakening to this divine gift and call in my life took place in the fall of 1990—a time of my feeling lost and my seeking to understand who I was and what I was called to do in pastoral ministry. That fall, early each morning, I would make my way to the family room and sit before a window that overlooked a birch tree in the front yard. I brought to this place a struggling faith and all the misgivings and terrors of my life. I resisted an urge to flee from that moment. Instead, I opened my prayer book. I prayed the prayer of the week. I read the psalm. I read the daily scripture with its accompanying spiritual reflection. I journaled.

Little by little I began to notice an inviting silence settle around my heart. Slowly I began to realize that this silence was the presence of God in my life. I also began to see that in this silence God was feeding a very deep need in my heart: my longing to be welcomed and accepted on my own terms. I longed to be known, to be understood. I longed to know, in the very deep, lonely place to which contemplative prayer had brought me, that I was not alone. Yes, in these moments of prayerful silence I would say God was accepting me on my terms and showing me who I might become on God's terms. Prodigal son that I was, God was giving me a hospitality that brought healing and new life to my soul.

I felt God, through these prayerful morning times, was visiting my heart, enlarging it, and calling me to a new kind of ministry. For five years I had no clear understanding of or name for the ministry to which I was being called. Kathleen Norris's writing helped clarify and define the ministry God calls me to offer. It is a ministry of hospitality that flows from and is totally dependent upon the hospitality God gives to me in the center of my heart.

What Are the Ways People Can Be Awakened?

I find it difficult to put aside my how-to mentality as I talk about this ministry. Something in me wants to jump to finding methods, leaving behind the place in my heart that is the source and guide for this ministry. James Finley helped me see that the ways reside in finding the right attitudes, not the right methods.

Finley has taught me that I first must take the time to cultivate an attitude of faith, openness, gratitude, attention, reverence, supplication, trust, joy, and expectation. To this litany of attitudes I would add hospitality. How can I offer a ministry of hospitality? Finley helps me see, "Cultivate an attitude of hospitality that is so deep I become a person of hospitality. In hospitality I discover how to offer a ministry of hospitality." Finley's counsel was to seek first the Holy Spirit and its fruit. When we allow the Spirit to transform our attitudes we will have found the way to awaken others to the divine longing.

On my bookshelf are books with the following titles: *A Spiritual Formation Workbook*; *Dreams and Spiritual Growth: A Christian Approach to Dreamwork Including 37 Dreamwork Techniques*; *How to Meditate without Leaving the World*; *The Story of Your Life: Writing a Spiritual Autobiography*. To this list I could also add my doctor of ministry paper, "Hidden Ache of the Heart," which includes the interview process designed to awaken people to their divine longing.

Each of the above contains useful tools for spiritual leaders to help people grow spiritually. Yet without something else, all of these can become manipulative gimmicks that block the awakening the spiritual leader really seeks. Helping people know and respond to the divine longing is never a matter of finding the right tool, method, or process. First and foremost it is a matter of the spiritual leader's finding the right self. The "right self" is always the inner Self, the spiritual leader's true self. Once we know and live hospitality, any one of the books listed above can become a marvelous means of offering hospitality.

The ministry of hospitality is a ministry of prayerful attentiveness, prayerful listening. The spiritual leader's listening to and tending to God's longing in himself or herself will enable the seeing and listening to the divine longing in another. The ministry of hospitality is a product of prayerful attention to God's hospitable presence both in the spiritual leader and in the other. To focus on a tool or method is to lose sight of who does the awakening. In short, the spiritual leader must become present to and involved with the person to whom he or she is ministering. A tool without a welcoming, hospitable gaze leaves untouched the deep yearning of the heart.

An attitude of faith, openness, gratitude, attentiveness, reverence, trust, joy, expectation, and hospitality becomes all-important. Only then might you turn (or not turn) to the tools in the books. Offer one or just be a hospitable presence to the other.

Rueben Job, in his lecture entitled "Spirituality: The Way," makes the same point as Finley. Job says there are no methods or systems *per se* of spiritual growth. Then he turns to the John Wesley Covenant Prayer, which in United Methodist circles is a rich prayer of commitment to Christ Jesus.

> I am no longer my own, but thine.
> Put me to what thou wilt, rank me with whom thou wilt.
> Put me to doing, put me to suffering.
> Let me be employed by thee or laid aside for thee,
> exalted for thee or brought low by thee.
> Let me be full, let me be empty.
> Let me have all things, let me have nothing.
> I freely and heartily yield all things
> to thy pleasure and disposal.
> And now, O glorious and blessed God,
> Father, Son, and Holy Spirit,
> thou art mine, and I am thine. So be it.
> And the covenant which I have made on earth,
> let it be ratified in heaven.[10]

By lifting up this covenant prayer, Job led me to see that the church offers the spiritual leader a concrete symbol for engaging people in a ministry of divine longing. The symbol is the covenant Christ makes with believers at our baptism, a covenant that is continually nurtured, deepened, and expanded through the Eucharist. I believe the sacraments, with their divine covenant, furnish a spiritual leader an arena to engage people in a ministry of divine longing. Certainly one way to view the sacraments is as manifestations of God's longing for us and our longing for God.

Thus from contemporary spiritual writers I gleaned rich insights and kindred conclusions about our common quest for the divine longing. I experienced change and counsel, both of which have guided me to see and offer my ministry in new ways.

C h a p t e r   5

EXPERIENCING
THE LONGING
IN MINISTRY

*This giddy sweetness [of Benedictine hospitality] may
still be found in American monasteries, though the language is toned down. It has deep roots in the notion of
God's ever-present hospitality in both nature and other
people, the idea that, properly understood, everything in
creation invites us to share in God's love. A story that eloquently expresses this may be found in the life of Benedict
himself. It is said that a priest came unexpectedly to the
saint's cave, bringing food. "Let us eat," he said, "for it is
Easter." Benedict replied, "I know that it is Easter, for I
have been granted the blessing of seeing you."* [1]

—KATHLEEN NORRIS, *DAKOTA*

Kathleen Norris describes how experiencing the stable,
bare-bones existence of a monastery gives one the chance
to change and to "redefine success as an internal process rather
than an outward display of wealth and power." [2] I would hardly
call my recent appointment to a two-point rural charge as being
assigned to a bare-bones existence. I would, however, see it as a
place of "stability" where I have been given the opportunity to
do exactly what Ms. Norris did in the monastery.

Receiving an appointment in the United Methodist sys-
tem is a reality check like no other on the desires of the heart
of a United Methodist pastor. I was shocked into numbness
when I got the call from the district superintendent: "Well,
Thad, we have an appointment for you. It is a two-point
charge: Oakfield…" He said the name of the second church,
but shock blocked my hearing its name. This was certainly not
a place of prestige to conclude my ministry. (None of my
friends knew where it was.) But then came a sequence of
divine nudges and awakenings in my heart that pointed me to
another kind of glory and success.

First, later that evening as I lay on the couch attempting to
prayerfully piece this together as I read the spiritual journal
Weavings, my older son came over to me and said, "Dad, I was
going to write you a note, but since you're still up I'll tell you.
I can't tell you how much respect I have for you for the way
you have responded to this appointment." Healing balm for
my bruises! I continued to read with my wife sitting across the
room and my son behind me. As I did, I heard a barely audible
voice inside me saying, *I am a fortunate man,…I am a fortunate
man.* The words were not a contrived ego pump-up. They were
a revelation from the Self in me who longs to be faithful to
God's call and is detached from concerns about United
Methodist cabinet appointments.

Second came a meeting with the superintendent of the district to which I was being appointed. Despite my son's affirmation, the disappointment I felt continued to take a toll. The
superintendent was a trusted friend, yet I approached the meeting feeling weary and depressed. I bared my soul to her. I shared
my shock and confusion. She listened. She understood and
sympathized. At my request, she told me honestly the reasons

she felt this was a good appointment for me: the profile of what the churches were looking for in a pastor matched my gifts and interests in ministry; and when this appointment came up for consideration, she had experienced a strong nudge of the Spirit with my name on it. We cried together. For reasons I still do not understand, I began to feel a peace and excitement about this appointment. I felt that the tears, the peace, and the excitement were stirrings of the Holy Spirit. I left the meeting energized and optimistic. The only reason I can give is that I awakened and responded to God's longing for me and my longing for God.

Following that I attended a meeting with the Pastor-Parish Relations Committee of Oakfield and Eden-Tabor Parish. I would describe it as a hospitable meeting. For reasons I do not entirely understand, I felt very much at home with these small-town, rural people. That night I sensed God's invitation to offer the ministry I'd been given in this place.

What are the ways a pastor can awaken people to respond to God's longing for them and their longing for God? My experience gave me three important clues to the foundation for this ministry. First: Believe! Something in my soul had been formed enough to believe I am a fortunate man because I know God longs for me and I long for God. Second: Pay attention! I paid attention to these "obscure" happenings that revealed to me my "little secret love," "my inmost Self" that is Christ's heart in mine. Third: Obey! I obeyed and embraced what God had given me. I obeyed my call, not my career aspirations. The message was clear: Believe, pay attention, obey the voice that tells me I am a fortunate man to be the pastor of Oakfield and Eden-Tabor United Methodist Parish and calls me to offer God's hospitality to the wonderful people there.

In my first seven months, my believing, paying attention, and obeying have prepared me to minister with a heart full of hospitality and delight in who these people are. I do not know from whence comes this delight. It simply comes into my heart as I live with them as their pastor. I know my task is not to know why but simply to believe, pay attention to, and obey this gift which God so mysteriously has placed in my heart.

Delight: Path to Awakening the Longing

In this delight, I am finding the ways to awaken people to respond to the divine longing. Three events from the Christmas holidays of 1995 will illustrate.

The first event occurred on Christmas morning. We planned the service, which fell on a Sunday that year, around Christmas carols. The carols filled the sanctuary with the wonder and joy of God's presence in our hearts through Christ's birth. At the conclusion of the service, one woman came out, handed me a gift, gave me a hug, and said, "Thank you for the joy you have brought into my life!" I was startled and humbled by the comment. How had I done that?

I stopped myself. Did I have to know how? No, I simply needed to accept, believe, heed, and obey the truth the woman was sharing with me. In some way, she had seen the joy of God's hospitality in me and was now returning the gift. I heard the instruction: "Cultivate an attitude of joy. Let joy become so deep you become a person of joy. It is in the joy that you shall find what this ministry is and the way to offer it."

The second incident occurred during an in-depth faith interview I held with a woman for her spiritual guidance. It proved to be a deeply moving exercise for her. I mention the experience, though, because of its effect on me, one that is a bit difficult to describe. I asked the same questions I had in other interviews. I did the same careful and accepting listening. I followed up when she offered significant disclosures. This woman got in touch with important life events. She appeared to have a fuller understanding of herself and her relationship with God.

The change was not in what I did but in my understanding of what I did. I realized that what made this an effective process was not primarily the questions but the presence of hospitality I offered in the interview process through the questions.

The third incident was a telephone call I made to a woman on a church matter. Near the conclusion of the conversation, the woman thanked me for the Christmas gift and note on my card that I had given her. In it I told her how much I appreciated the gift of ministry she brought to our congregation and me. Tearfully she said, "I can't tell you how good it feels to be appreciated." The feeling in her words moved and awakened me to see what I had really done when I expressed honest words of appreciation to this woman. Unknowingly I had given to her what I have come to see God gives to me in the prayerful silence of contemplation: appreciation, recognition, acceptance of who I am and the gifts I have to give. My gesture of appreciation stirred in her an awakened sense of who she was as a valued human being.

Through these events, I saw the truth of Kathleen Norris's conclusion that genuine success was accomplished internally, not in showy displays of money and influence. I believe through learning to believe, pay attention, and obey, God is showing me new ways to see ministry and myself in ministry. In surprising ways, God is awakening me to respond to God's longing in others and in me. I am most grateful.

THE LONGING IN THE LIVES OF PARISHIONERS

*As applied to Christian life we can observe a universal
contemplative dimension to our faith. Every Christian
experiences at least a momentary taste of the need to be
with God in a childlike, silent awareness of his loving
presence. There is in the heart of every disciple the need to
touch, however obscurely, a depth of simple communion
with our Lord "closer to us than we are to ourselves."*[1]

—JAMES FINLEY

I would now like to tell the story of exploring the nature of
the divine longing in the lives of the parishioners in the
church in Milwaukee. First I shall describe the interview process
I used and what I learned about the ways my parishioners awakened to God's longing for them and their longing for God.
Then I shall share the interview responses of two of the eighteen people. I also shall share what I learned about the role a
spiritual leader may play in persons' awakening to the divine
longing.

The Interview Process

I began with a scripture conversation, using John 21. I read
aloud a passage from Henri Nouwen's book *In the Name of*

Jesus in which Nouwen described God's incarnate heart being in our hearts. I told the participants that I was interested in exploring this dimension of their hearts with them and in hearing the ways in which they had awakened to God's presence in their lives. I then instructed them,

> Recall times God has "strangely warmed your heart," times you have wakened to God's love for you and your love for God. Consider childhood moments, times of crisis, times you were surprised by the joy of God's presence, times of searching, and seminar and retreat experiences. Include turning points, breakthrough moments, and less dramatic daily nudges, such as over coffee with a friend, listening to music in solitude, at work, in your garden, with your hobby, in worship, and so forth.

I left them alone to reflect upon and write their response. When they were finished, I then said,

> Reflect upon and journal the thoughts, the feelings, the desire God stirred in your heart at these times. Such stirrings often come in the form of an image, a sense of deep inner silence, a certain intuitive knowing. Try to capture in words, word pictures, or phrases what God awakened in your heart.

Again I left them alone to reflect and write their response.

During the next phase of the interview they shared with me what they uncovered with the first two questions. I then asked the following questions and recorded their responses:

- In these moments when you awakened to God's desire for you and your desire for God, what do you believe God has given to you which you long to share with others? Another way to talk about this is to share which spiritual gifts you feel God has given you.

- As you look at your experiences, what are the ways God seems to awaken you to respond to God's longing for you and your longing for God?

- What do you do that nourishes your awareness and response to God's presence and call? What within and around you draws you away from faithful response to God? In other words, what do you do that draws you into your desire for God? What inwardly and outwardly distracts you from this desire?

- In what ways does our church awaken and nourish your desire for God?

- Finally, what do you feel God is asking you to contribute to your church? to your world?

- What of value for you has occurred in this time together?

I then thanked them, and we ended the interview with a warm hug. The hug always seemed a natural and fitting way to bring closure to a time of such intimacy.

Two Stories I Heard

Jane

Both interviews I wish to highlight were with women. The first I shall call Jane. Jane is a middle-aged woman who grew up at Aldersgate and left it in her early adult years. She was a successful career woman who felt the need to return to her roots to care for her aging mother. She also felt the need to return to her home church.

Jane and her husband became regular attenders and both assumed leadership positions. In earlier pastoral visits I learned some of her story. She had struggled with and learned to overcome alcoholism. She had experienced two failed marriages. She also had had some rich encounters with God.

After Jane journaled her answers to my first questions, we

came back together. The following was her response to
Recall times God has strangely warmed your heart.

In 1959 when I was seven, I nearly died from scarlet fever.
I was so sick that nothing else mattered. I overheard my
parents saying that I might die. I was in my room in bed
when I found myself up above my body, and I didn't feel
any pain. It was like a shaft of light through me [the "me"
above her body]. I knew everything. I had all knowledge. I
had this incredible sense of love and oneness. I didn't know
what it was. There was a presence—God? Jesus? The Holy
Spirit? I don't know how long it lasted.

When I was eleven years old, my father had a nervous
breakdown. I felt like I was dead. That experience [of
when I was seven] came back to me. I felt connected. . . . I
belong!

In 1969, I knew before the call came that a relative had
died.

In high school I remember walking to church in the
snow on Christmas Eve…singing carols.… You felt swept
up into God. I could feel Jesus being born.

In 1983, 1984 I had gone through two marriages. I
was successful in my job, but I was empty. I realized I was
looking for love in all the wrong places. My backyard
overlooked a church. I sat at the window looking at people going to church. It was First United Methodist Church
of Birmingham. I started attending. I started to listen to
God's message, and I began to heal.

Getting my adopted son. R. is God's gift to me.

Flying home through a terrible storm, we broke
through the clouds. This great sense of peace came over me.

The return home to Milwaukee and re-relating to parents. When my father was dying he said, "Everything will
be okay."

Listening to the brook as I sit in my backyard. At night looking at the stars.

I had an experience in therapy—had an image of God holding me like a child . . . had a sense of his arms. I learned others cared. People were feeding me.

The music at church.

I asked Jane if she had ever told anyone about her out-of-body experience as an eleven-year-old. She told me that at the time she had tried to tell her parents. They discounted what she said as a delusion caused by the fever. "I never told another soul until now."

I have come to see that Jane's experience of not sharing—of being discouraged to share—is common. We live in a culture and church that indirectly, and often directly, hushes the exchange of such profound spiritual awakenings. I wonder what harm to people's souls and spiritual growth such discounting causes!

Jane's response to the second question, ***What does God stir in your heart?*** was as follows.

Total peace with the world and people…Totally safe… Totally loved…Totally protected….All-loving parent will protect me, no matter what is said or done….I feel one with God.

I don't care about any of the other stuff going on in my life. Things don't matter, resentments don't matter. Money doesn't matter. The only thing that matters is now. I feel enveloped in brightness and light. I know God is love. I must stay connected with others through this love.

I asked the next set of questions verbally. Here are Jane's answers.

What has God given you to share with others?

I want to share with others God's love. . . . I want them to turn into that, I want to lead others into that.

What are the ways God seems to awaken you?

I get to the point where there is no other place to turn...Repeating the Serenity Prayer...I turn to images.... I stop to be with God.

What do you do that nourishes you? distracts you?

Nature, music, seasons changing, people in crisis. Getting caught up in day-to-dayness of life.

In what ways does our church awaken and nourish you?

The stained-glass windows at church, the shaft of light through them. The choir. Louise [the choir director]. Sermons hit a chord. People sharing joys and concerns.

What do you feel God is asking you to contribute?

Chairing Vision Team.

What of value for you has occurred in this interview?

It's been a new way to look at the experiences of my life. It's helped me tie them together, identify.... I'm more aware, see how I am to do it.

I recall many rich observations and feelings from this interview. One, this is a woman who has been there and done many things. She became quite secular for a period, yet she says God never left her. That fact impresses me, as well as the number of ways this secular woman states she found awakening in her church.

Sally

The second woman's experience differs significantly from Jane's. Sally never left the church. She was always very active. At the time of the interview, she was the church school superintendent. Here is her response to

Recall times God has strangely warmed your heart.

As a little girl I attended a big Methodist church. One time I went with my grandmother into the choir room and stood beside her while she talked with a choir member. I had this wondrous feeling [that] I belonged. I belonged here.

At a Christmas Eve service when I was still a child, the picture of Jesus I saw deeply touched me.

Bible studies when the kids were small. Bob was working long hours. It was the early 1970s. At the Bible study God was beginning to touch me.

My involvement with Sunday school teaching. I learn along with the kids. Now I see the impact this is having.

At the Lay Witness Mission. At final worship service when there was an altar call, I told J. I wasn't going down. The next thing I knew I had this "force" driving me there. For the first time I wasn't afraid. It was so peace-filled. I felt so accepted. That Sunday there was that absolute knowing. It wasn't just a feeling; it was a knowing.

Stressful times with C. I was angry about this. I was making the bed and talking to God. I said, "I'm turning this whole thing over to you." A burden was lifted. I trusted God.

When I work with people, knowing God is with me.

What does God stir in your heart?

That time with my grandma was awe-filled, something I didn't understand. I felt accepted and loved, touched in a new way. [My life is] never dull, never boring.

What has God given you to share with others?

I look at things differently, defuse situations. Being a contemplative presence.

What are the ways God seems to awaken you?

The church school.

What do you do that nourishes you? distracts you?

Worship, church school, Bible studies.
Wanting my way, the busyness.

In what ways does our church awaken and nourish you?

All that has been mentioned. People who have similar beliefs—it's a family. It's an important place—the most important place. [It provides a] situation where I can grow: Bible studies and church school.

What do you feel God is asking you to contribute?

The word that comes to me is *expectation*. Not feeling guilty. I want to do something for others, reach out, go beyond self.

What for you of value has occurred in this interview?

Anything like this is good. It brings things up. Just being able to share is a wonderful experience.

So much that Sally said touched and impressed me. Two things stand out. The first was her awakening to God as a young girl in the choir room. I can picture the scene. The choir members are going through the routine of robing and preparing for the

Christmas Eve service. Unbeknownst to anyone present, Christ is being born in the little girl who stands with her grandmother—true Christmas magic, holy magic. I wonder how much I miss in the lives of children and adults. How often have I walked on holy ground and not seen the bush burning or not heard the invitation to take off my shoes?

The second thing that strikes me about Sally is the way that for her, church work was sacred work. She wasn't the superintendent because no one wanted the job, but because she awakened to God's longing for her and her longing for God in this labor of love. Sally bears witness to me that for so many church officers, what they do in the church is holy work. She reminds me to be respectful of and humbly grateful for people who experience God's presence in the work of the institutional church.

Though the interview project emerged from both professional and faith motivations, actually doing the interviews and reviewing the responses have led me from the professional aspect of parish ministry to its whole dimension. I feel humbled by the treasures of the heart that each of the eighteen people gave me. I feel awakened to the fact that in such a rich variety of ways, God has longed for these people and they, in previously undisclosed ways, have longed for God. The interviews have been deeply informing about the ways of God in the lives of average parishioners. And for me as a pastor, they have been a way to awaken God's longing for me and my longing for God.

INSIGHTS FROM THE INTERVIEWS

*While at one level remaining quite distinct, the experi-
ence of sitting in meditation and the experience of being
with others come together as two manifestations of one
divine call—to say yes to each new, unexpected mani-
festation of love. Always the movement is the same—
yielding again and again to the freedom of the eternal
Someone who forever calls us to himself, now in this
moment of silent prayer, now in this moment with others. . . . Both the silence of our prayer and the nearest
thou at hand lure us into an ever more faithful following
of the divine call to die to ourselves so as to be born into
the Love that is our life.*[1]

—JAMES FINLEY

As I said in the previous chapter, the interview experience
pleased and informed me in a significant way as a minister. I'd like to share here the discoveries I found through my
parishioners' experiences. I asked the following questions:
*What is the nature of the longing and how does it manifest itself in
the lives of people? What are the ways people awaken to the divine
longing? What can I, as pastor, be and do to awaken people to respond
to God's desire for them and theirs for God?*

Gleanings on the Nature of the Divine Longing

Seeking to know the nature of the divine longing is like seeking to know the nature of Beethoven's Ninth Symphony. The real answer comes in the hearing. What I heard in my parishioners' answers revealed much. Listen carefully to their words:

> Questions, confusion…hunger… scared…What do I do with my life?…Sad, happy, glad, awe…tears that I was connected with God. It is like opening a closed-up house in the spring.
>
> Total peace with the world and people…totally safe…loved.…I don't care about any of the stuff going on in my life…resentments, money…Only thing that matters is now. I feel enveloped in brightness and light.
>
> Like a little child, [with] the curiosity of a little child. I wonder why I'm having a vision—why me?
>
> Awe-filled…accepted and loved…belonging…touched in a new way. [Life is] never dull, never boring.
>
> Despair. Comfort. Listened to. Supported. Called. Surprised. Rejuvenated. Excited. Elated.
>
> Facing, breaking the fear barrier…learning to trust…real separation and reunion.

What these words revealed to me about the nature of the longing was, namely, that we know the longing through words that are heartfelt utterances. Through his book *The Sacred Journey*, word-craftsman and novelist Frederick Buechner helps me understand the significance of what occurred as I heard these accounts of people's awakenings:

> This teacher, Mr. Martin, was the first to give me a feeling for what words are, and can do, in themselves. Through him I started to sense that words have color, depth, texture of their own, and the power to evoke vastly more than

they mean; that words can be used not merely to make things clear, make things vivid, make things interesting and whatever else, but to make things happen inside the one who reads them or hears them.[2]

This list of holy stirrings, words of potency and poignancy, points to something "more than they mean" inside the people who shared them. As one who listened to and recorded them, I discover that the people's words do indeed have a power to "make something happen inside the one who...hears them." That something is the igniting of the divine longing.

These words give us windows into the nature of the divine longing in those who uttered them and also in those of us who read the list. This is evident by what happens in my heart when I reread them: I feel the awakening of a clean, open space within me. I feel awe. I feel wonder at the gift given to me by God through these people. I feel humbled and challenged, and gratitude. I feel love for these people...tenderness...assurance. My faith is nurtured. My life direction and ministry are affirmed. I feel a silent, unseen holy presence settle in and around me.

Several thoughts strike me here: First, understanding the nature and truth of the divine longing is simply not a spectator sport! We only understand words that express the divine longing when we let these words wake in us an awareness of God's longing for us and ours for God. There simply are no outside, neutral observers to this truth of God's dwelling in our hearts. We know the nature of the divine longing when words, people, and events lead us to know in faith:

O Lord, you have searched me and known me. (Ps. 139:1)

As a deer longs for flowing streams,
    so longs my soul for you, O God. (Ps. 42:1)

> O God…my soul thirsts for you…
>   as in a dry and weary land where there is no water.
>   (Ps. 63:1)

The other thing I notice is the kind of language necessary to speak of and understand the divine longing. This language is often missing when church people discuss matters of faith and God. I believe that we as the church should be conversant in several kinds of speech. We need a language of the institution, a functional parlance that describes the tangible elements of ministry, such as job definitions, committee functions, program goals, methods for doing programs. We also need a language of speculative theology, which helps us define such key concepts as sin, redemption, Christ, God, salvation, grace, and so on.

In the work of these interviews, I discovered the need for a third language: one of the Spirit. The stirrings I recorded used words of poetry, metaphor, touch, silence, and story. This language has the power to evoke far more than the words literally mean. And as I said, the language of the Spirit often goes unnoticed or unused by a church whose seminaries prize intellectual clarity and whose local bodies and conferences become preoccupied with institutional matters. The results of my interviews confirm that if we are to experience and understand God's presence beyond us and in us, church leaders and pastors need to invite, honor, and employ a language of the Spirit. No other language can translate the experience of the divine longing into understanding. This language creates awareness of what otherwise goes unseen and disregarded, to our soul's detriment.

Gleanings on the Impact of the Longing

In the lives of those interviewed, we can see that the longing had the following effects:

- A sense of God's hand in life. People saw God less as a remote deity and more as a divine presence he/she meets in life events.
- A sense of God in the ordinary. One woman related how she met "the extraordinary in the ordinary": "It is in the things that happen naturally. I'm making the bed, I see the sunlight peeking through the trees. I see the Lord. He is there. I give thanks."
- A sense of purpose in life. Many felt reassured or stimulated to think about their places and/or vocations.
- A sense of God-given ability. Several talked about gaining an awareness of the skills and gifts God had given them and feeling a desire to use them.
- A sense of God's immense love and a wish to share that love. Almost all of those interviewed expressed this. "God has given me eyes to see. I wish I could push the blinders back so they could see." "[I want to] defuse situations… be a contemplative presence." "I wish to share my compassion for the unfortunate." "[I want to] give undeserved love… surprise others with God's generosity." "I think I have a real message to frightened people that the fire does not eat you up. I trust God will be there for me…for you. We shall not remain the same."

When people awaken to God's longing for them, they want to live in this love and give to others what they have received. It isn't a new finding, yet these reportings are a fresh reminder of the impact of the Holy when we connect with God at the deepest level.

Gleanings about Awakening to the Longing

I realize that the ways in which people awaken to God's presence are, as the psalmist says, "more than the sand." The following lists ways I heard in the interviews. Although not exhaustive, it is informative.

- Life crisis—family difficulty, job loss, death of a loved one, divorce, serious illness, or death of a friend
- Other people—either receiving love from or giving love to others
- Personal prayer—reading the Bible, meditating, intentional times of solitude with God
- Retreats—a planned time away with others in a Christian setting
- Church activities—including performing some task in the church such as teaching church school, serving on a committee, working on a program
- Worship services—Sunday morning worship, Christmas Eve, Easter
- Music—church or other
- Church atmosphere—being alone in a church building
- Small groups—prayer groups or Bible study
- Times in nature—taking walks, being in a park, forest, or by a body of water, usually alone
- Special family events—reunions, weddings, anniversaries, births, adoptions
- Sermons
- Personal health crisis
- Reading
- Sacraments/Confirmation
- Counseling
- Children
- Prayer amidst daily challenges—job stress or turmoil
- Dreams

- Meeting the extraordinary in the ordinary—confronted by the Holy in everyday events
- Other people praying
- Social justice issues
- The arts—other than music

The responses in this list appear in order of frequency. The respondents mentioned "life crisis" twenty-two times, "other people" nineteen times, "personal prayer" and "retreats" fourteen times each. The rest had an even distribution. We might divide the list into categories: general life experience, settings of the church life, settings of personal prayer practice, and settings of pastoral involvement.

What may these interview findings teach us about the ways people awaken to the divine longing? First, as I've emphasized throughout this book, God is the awakener. God is at work in the life and love and care of other people! Second, awakenings come when people have intentionally stepped aside or been forced to step aside from their routines. One can clearly see why "Remember the sabbath day, and keep it holy" (Exod. 20:8) is one of the Ten Commandments. Without times apart, we forget the saving truth that God longs for us and our hearts long for God.

Third, symbols, practices, and activities of the church do have the power to awaken people. This is a happy conclusion when we live in a time of such church disillusionment. I too get numbed by the bickering and boredom of many church meetings, the jokes and criticism about preaching, and the commercialism of the holy days. But so many respondents cited times when church activities, worship and prayer experiences, and church holy days were significant moments of awakening.

The fourth observation flows from the preceding. Though we spiritual leaders are not the awakener, we can play a key role in persons' awakenings. We can help people see, name, and understand the activity of God in their lives. We can be important guides in the way they respond to the Holy Spirit's stirring.

Gleanings about the Pastoral Role and Task

I am reminded of the Woody Allen line, "Ninety percent of success is in just showing up." Certainly ninety percent of success in this ministry is showing up with the faith that God is present. I can hear God almost shouting at me (or any spiritual leader), "You can have a role in my work. But I do the awakening. The best way you can do this ministry is to trust that I long to awaken people and I have made them to long to be awakened!"

This being so, what are the ways a spiritual leader can go about this work? I found revelations in how the respondents described the interview. They said the experience was

- a time of soul-searching and self-examination.
- a time to recall important memories.
- a time to sense who they were, their connection with God and God's with them.
- a time to touch, name, and share feelings.
- a time of spiritual motivation.
- a time of awareness.
- a time of healing.
- a time to make better sense of life.
- a time to share important matters of the heart with another.

Clearly the interview was a time when people awakened to

God. What then did I do to help this happen? Upon reflection, I see that I did the following:

1 I invited them to step aside from the routines of their lives.

2 I created a hospitable climate through scripture, conversation, prayer, and my attitude.

3 I asked sensitive, inviting, and challenging questions about their lives and relationships with God.

4 I helped them name and affirm the ways God was with them.

5 And I was a hospitable presence who listened and helped them honor, deepen, and discern their awareness of their lives' experiences and God's presence and movement in those experiences.

An Invitation to Step Aside

I believe the "awakenings" I have listed occurred because I asked people to step aside from their daily concerns, their problems, and church business. I designed this as a time for them to listen to what was in their hearts. Setting aside all the urgent matters of their lives for a period of time allowed them to become aware of their life journeys and God's (often surprising) presence in those journeys. This stepping aside awakened them to recognize which life demands and routines distracted them from seeing: God constantly has been longing for them, and their hearts have been longing for God.

The interviews were intense stepping-aside times. However, stepping aside can take the form of prayer before and during a committee meeting. It can come in a scripture and prayer during a hospital or home visit. It can come in the form of inviting a person or a group to see their experience and what they can do in a new way, such as from God's perspective. It is crucial to remember how routines can be blinding, and stepping aside can create potential for seeing. Maybe the most relevant thing we can do as ministers is encourage people to take time to be irrelevant in a holy, prayerful way.

A Hospitable Climate

We learned from Kathleen Norris's experience that she awakened to God when the monks offered her a prayerful, hospitable climate. She also noted that the hospitality she received flowed from the monks' prayer life. Key here is the rooting of spiritual leaders' lives in prayer, while allowing God's hospitality to create an attitude of welcome toward all we encounter. In short, if you want to offer the awakening experience to those you serve, pray unceasingly and welcome constantly!

Sensitive Questions

A spiritual leader in this kind of ministry is not primarily trying to impart doctrine, insight, or scriptural truths, though these are legitimate and important elements of ministry. A spiritual leader's real aim is to invite people to look at and listen to their life experiences, to realize the ways God has touched their hearts, and to uncover their heart's hidden ache for God. Prayer-rooted questions are a tool for this work. Such questions are not analytical or designed to get people to see a particular point. The questions are open-ended and theological, designed to awaken people to discover what the Spirit wants them to see.

I find this process particularly applicable when I relate to people in crisis. I have learned that I need not only to be supportive but discerning. I need to distinguish the ways God is present and is speaking to the sufferer in his or her pain. That means we encourage people to enter and go through their pain instead of running from or just "getting over" it. And that entails a trust that God is present in the pain to heal and make new.

Affirmation of God's Presence

Quite often I have watched people's pleasurable surprise when
I would name the presence of God in an experience they had.
They would say in a grateful way, "I didn't think about that as
experiencing God." One of the most moving reactions came
when one woman told me, "Until this interview, I did not
believe I was worthy of a relationship with God!"

Because of the theological dualism so long present in the
church, people have been trained to see God's activities only in
church services and activities and not in their daily experiences. I believe an important element in this kind of ministry
is helping people discern and name the holy moments God
gives them. By discerning, affirming, and naming such
moments, a spiritual leader consecrates their lives and experiences. This refreshes their perspective, allowing them to see
God not only in hymn or prayer but in the office, the barn-
yard, the coffee shop, the family meal, and so on.

A Hospitable Presence

The fifth factor is not something I did, but something I was led
to become. In the interviews I became a hospitable presence.
Perhaps it is more accurate to say that I responded to God's call
to become a hospitable presence. I don't think such a role is
anything any of us can decide to do as we might decide, for
instance, to be a friendly host at a gathering or a friendly pastor
to our congregation. Both have their place. But to become a
hospitable presence, one who awakens people to the divine
longing, is a role only God can give and call us to assume.

Furthermore, I believe that being led to assume this role is
the key element in the way a spiritual leader awakens people
to God's longing for them and their longing for God. In other
words, the primary power in this ministry was not in what I

did, but in what I was led to become. Inviting people to step aside, the hospitable climate, the sensitive, challenging questions, and the naming and affirming of God's presence were all quite important. But they flowed from what God wanted me to become. I believe the hospitable presence I assumed invited and encouraged people to awaken to God's presence in their lives and share that presence with me.

In the next chapter, I talk about this role and what is required for a spiritual leader to be God's hospitable presence in her or his ministry.

LIVING IN THE SILENCE

Happy are they who know that their heart cries out from a wilderness; and silence blossoms on their lips.
—ABRAHAM YITCHAK

I call this chapter "Living in the Silence" because I know that when I faithfully live in the silence of God, I am a hospitable presence to others. By living in that contemplative silence, I glean the grace to offer to people a litany of things they need:

A joy, delight, and interest in who they are.

A welcoming, safe place where they can let their feelings, thoughts, and longings emerge and be shared.

A love that listens to the "silent" movement of the Spirit in their lives.

A nondefensiveness and openness when in conflict with them.

A desire to offer to them the shalom of God, which invites them to know and awaken to the divine longing.

Living in the silence does not mean ceasing to speak. Rather it is an inner posture of prayer in which I allow space for God's heart to become incarnate in my heart. It is not hyperbole but a mystery of faith to say that when I live in the silence, I become host for the Holy Spirit. My personhood becomes Christ's sacrament to others when my heart answers God's call to dwell in God's silence; to offer God's delights, friendship, mercy, and healing to others.

It is also not hyperbole to say that I feel very much a beginner, a struggler at living in the silence in the way God has given and unceasingly calls me to live. Therefore I wish to explore more fully here what God requires of me to live in the silence as God's hospitable presence—in my pastor's world of weekly sermon, Bible-study preparation, confirmation class, unexpected telephone calls, surprising anger from parishioners, equally surprising love from parishioners, hospital calls, home visits....you can complete the list.

Know Your Human Limits

The first requirement is to accept the lesson that the school of hard knocks in ministry teaches: This ministry is humanly impossible! It requires taking to heart the lesson that Jesus taught his first seminary students. "Children, how hard it is to enter the kingdom of God! It is easier for a camel to go through the eye of a needle than for someone who is rich [for example, a seminarian] to enter the kingdom of God." His students wanted to know, "Then who can be saved?" And so do we! Then comes Jesus' punch line: "For mortals it is impossible, but not for God; for God all things are possible" (Mark 10:24-27). I imagine Jesus said that with a knowing smile.

In other words, living in the silence calls upon us to believe the unbelievable. Often it seems unbelievable that the Holy Spirit is living in my heart, a heart filled with so many voices, so much guilt, and so many strivings. Therefore, living in the silence requires that I tenaciously believe the voice of prayer who speaks to me amidst the anguish and doubt of my life. I hear this amazing, steadfast presence inside me saying, *Thad, trust that I can break the evil spell of your aimless busyness. Trust that I want only to be with you. Let go of your anxious schemes. Let go of your self-doubt and self-hate. Let go of your unbelief that I am not with you. Let's you and I go to the silent place where we can enjoy each other, befriend each other, and live in the unspeakable peace and love that God eternally affords.*

I hear this voice when I set time aside to read scripture prayerfully and to let Christ guide me to this silent presence within. That is a requirement! But I have come to see that more is required than setting aside time to pray.

Listen to the Longing

I realize also that I need to heed the Spirit's invitation for me to pray unceasingly. I need to train my mind and heart to listen constantly to the divine longing.

When I practice this contemplative listening in both my praying and living, I experience what the author of Ephesians expressed when he wrote, "[There is] one Lord, one faith, one baptism, one God and Father of all, who is above all and through all and in all" (Eph. 4:5-6). Through such listening, I have come to realize the truth the psalmist uttered: "Where can I go from your spirit? Or where can I flee from your presence? / If I ascend to heaven, you are there; if I make my bed in Sheol, you are there" (Ps. 139:7-8).

Refer to Others' Wisdom

Constant contact with the wisdom of others is another requirement for living in the silence. The witness of sister and brother pilgrims through both personal and written encounters draws me into the silence. One such pilgrim, a woman I met only briefly, impacted me greatly through her writing about living in the silence as she lay dying of cancer. In the summer 1989 issue of *Haelen*, the late Dr. Lee Morical spoke of the victory that Christ gives to those who trust his life-giving presence even in the cold quiet of death: "I learned that it is not in the getting and having it all, but in the letting go, that we begin to find the peace which passes all understanding. And it is only when we realize that life has no safety nets—never had, never will—that we begin to know that out of God's love we cannot fall."

I am discovering, that living in the silence requires a trust in the revelation God gives in the silence of contemplative prayer: "There are no safety nets—never have been, never will be. Trust, Thad, that out of my love you cannot fall." I was given to see this saving truth several years ago through a dream and ensuing journal dialogue.

The dream stems from a moment in my life when I harshly discovered that there are, truly, no safety nets in life. As I mentioned earlier, at age fourteen, I was in a head-on car collision that killed a passenger in our vehicle and seriously injured my father and me. My front teeth were smashed, and my left leg was shattered at the thigh. But toughest of all for me at fourteen was the stark realization that the safety net of my father's love could not protect me from the terror of death.

I lived well into my adult years with this horror unresolved in my life. Then several years ago I had the following dream and journaled this dialogue. This dialogue brought the mysterious assurance of faith to my dread of a life void of safety nets. Its unfolding revealed that I could not fall outside of God's love. In the dream,

> I visit the city of the accident, Goldsboro, North Carolina, for a seminar on healing. I sit in the front of the church,

apart from everyone else. The seminar leader is a priest whose countenance is filled with the healing light of God. I am present as a professional who wants to learn the art of healing, yet another part of me—the lost-in-terror part of me—has come to be healed. Suddenly this part of me appears on the chancel steps in the exact condition I was in at fourteen when I arrived at the hospital. My leg is bloody. I feel unbearable pain. I am naked in terror.

Boy: (*horrified, afraid of death, feeling totally isolated*) I'm here—I can be seen, by nurses, my dad, my mother. But what I'm really feeling, what I really need and want are invisible. But I don't feel invisible to you!

Priest: You aren't!

Boy: Becoming invisible must be what it feels like to die.

Priest: Do you feel as if you are dying?

Boy: I don't know. I'm losing blood. That pain in my leg is unbearable. My breath is gone from me. . . . You are breathing for me?

Priest: Yes, I am.

Boy: In the invisible place, you are with me, breathing new life into what feels terrifying.

Priest: Yes, I am.

This dialogue reminds me of John's account of what happened to the disciples on Easter evening. I felt the same comfort, and from the same source.

> When it was evening on that day, the first day of the week, and the doors of the house where the disciples had met were locked for fear of the Jews, Jesus came and stood among them and said, "Peace be with you." After he said this, he showed them his hands and his side. Then the disciples rejoiced when they saw the Lord. Jesus said to them

again, "Peace be with you. As the Father has sent me, so I send you." When he had said this, he breathed on them and said to them, "Receive the Holy Spirit" (John 20:19-22).

Know That Easter Is True

The final requirement, which is also the first requirement for living in the silence, is not just believing but knowing that Easter is true! Of course God gives this gift to all through Christ. But I have come to see, as I struggle to live in the silence, that the gift comes with a requirement. Even as I write, I know in the hidden silence of my heart (and of the world) that God is giving to his son Thad (and to the world), the love that even death cannot silence. And God is asking of his son Thad (and the world): "Let go of your conviction that you can find some permanent safety net—in career, success, pension, security, family love, or congregational approval. Trust in my son, Jesus Christ. Come live with him and others in the silence where my love reigns forever."

LIFE LESSONS ON THE LONGING

But just as we have the same spirit of faith that is in accordance with scripture—"I believed, and so I spoke"—we also believe, and so we speak, because we know that the one who raised the Lord Jesus will raise us also with Jesus, and will bring us with you into his presence.

—2 CORINTHIANS 4:13-14

Writing this book has given me important glimpses into understanding the nature of a pastoral ministry rooted in contemplative prayer. I have been practicing for two years what I've conveyed in the previous chapters: my learnings about living such a ministry and through it awakening parishioners to the divine longing and their longing for God. In this final chapter I would like to speak to the question: *What does it mean to faithfully live this contemplative call as a local church pastor?* For me in essence this question asks, *What does it mean to respond faithfully to God's longing for me and my longing for God in my life and in my ministry?*

First and foremost, it has meant yielding to the fact that my heart's longing for God has a purpose all its own. This holy longing, which is Christ's purpose and presence in me, continually judges and heals the lost and empty purpose of my life. I experience this healing in three ways: The divine longing 1) reminds, 2) draws, and 3) reveals.

The Reminding

The longing reminds me that God's desire for my life and the core desire of my heart are unspeakable blessings. It is unspeakable in the sense that no words can adequately describe this holy presence who lives both beyond and in my heart. I call these longings *blessings* because that word best describes the activity of the divine longing.

According to Webster's, *bless* means "to set apart or consecrate for holy purpose...to make happy...[or] successful...to wish happiness on...to consecrate by prayer...to praise; to magnify; to extol...to make the sign of the cross upon...to keep; guard; preserve." I experience the divine longing's continually reminding me of a holy purpose in my life. The longing brings immeasurable happiness to my heart and gives me the desire to want happiness for others. The divine longing is the consecrated prayer of the Holy Spirit in my life. It stirs praise and new openness to God and others. It is the judgment and mercy of Christ's cross upon my life, and in my prayers it guards and preserves my life.

I need the longing's reminding because I forget what God longs to offer and what my heart longs to receive. The divine longing breaks the spell of spiritual amnesia that is part and parcel of my daily life. When the longing awakens me, I hear a holy whisper: "Though you forget me, Thad, I do not forget you. I will not forget you or my world. Come live in the world in my eternal love." To hear this whisper in the center of my heart is to know that my life and all of life is an unspeakable blessing.

The Drawing

The divine longing draws me through prayer into my heart. I find myself being pulled to a wilderness place where I do not choose to go on my own. I am drawn to make this inner pilgrimage for a purpose: to learn to see the Real.

In the wilderness I realize how I let fear and shame determine what I see and want in my life. The divine longing unceasingly draws me within to teach my wounded and sin-flawed heart this truth: "Perfect love casts out fear" (1 John 4:18). When I allow myself to go into this place, I always find that the ill-begotten purposes and motivations of my life meet a healing, merciful love that does indeed cast out my fears and heal my shame. Drawn by God's longing for me and mine for God, I am given to see for myself the truth of Easter: Death is real—my death is real—but God's love in the risen Christ Jesus is stronger than death.

Through prayerful reading of scripture, dreams, worship, the writings of faithful pilgrims, intimate conversations with spiritual friends, and meeting the extraordinary in the ordinary I am given to see the Real. The Real is God's love beyond and in all creation—including me. The divine longing draws me into this hidden truth.

The Revealing

Earlier I said that the longing reminds me that God's desire for my life is unspeakable blessing. The primary aspect of this blessing is newfound purpose for my life. A dream I had several years ago illustrates this.

In the dream I am living in Kenosha, Wisconsin. I am planning to visit Appleton, some ninety miles away, to attend a school for United Methodist pastors. As I drive north, suddenly the highway is torn up for new construction. So I leave my car and begin walking determinedly. A friendly stranger joins me, trying to make conversation. I am too obsessed with my desire to reach Appleton to talk to him. Undaunted, the stranger persistently invites me to see a scene beyond the construction embankment nearby. I finally agree and stop walking to climb the hill. I am not prepared for what meets my eyes: a valley filled with what I can best describe as a sacred blue hue. *This is the valley of God's shalom,* I tell myself. *This is in me!*

But Appleton calls. I climb down and resume my trip.

Through this dream God gave me the opportunity to see a new purpose for my life. My dogged journey to Appleton reveals the ill-begotten purpose I was acting upon: to find significance and meaning through professional achievement. I believe the mysterious stranger was actually the holy Counselor, inviting me instead to see and desire a life-giving purpose: the presence of God's reign alive in my heart. When I awakened from the dream, my heart sang in blessing; I knew I was capable of desiring God's way in my life. And this was the fruit of the longing: to be showed and given the capacity to heed and follow God's way in my life.

The preceding begins to express some of what it means to respond faithfully to the diving longing. What does this heeding and following bring to my life and ministry? As Dr. Biersdorf indicated in the Foreword, my personal life has been difficult this year. In April I discovered I had prostate cancer, and in July, my house and one of the churches I serve were destroyed by an F5 tornado. I am still sorting through what all these events mean, but something is quite clear: by heeding and following the divine longing's reminding, drawing, and revealing, I have received four gifts.

The Gift of Deepened Faith

After thirty-three years in ordained ministry, I've obviously had many moments in which I have experienced "gifts of faith." But doesn't faith in one sense always come to us as a fresh gift? It certainly did for me the night I went to bed knowing I had a life-threatening illness.

I sat alone on the edge of my bed. I said aloud, "I have prostate cancer." I pondered, *This is big...too big for me....Don't try to "spiritual insight" your way through this one....I don't have the strength to face and beat this alone.*

Was I praying? I thought I had been thinking. Because of what next happened, I now feel that Someone in me was praying. Right after I confessed, "I don't have the strength," I started seeing faces, a parade of faces of people who loved me: my family, close friends, and parishioners. I thought, *There is where I'll find the strength! I don't have to face this alone. Let them in. Let their love carry me in my dark valley of the shadow of death.*

I successfully "feared no evil"—for about two hours! Then I awakened. The demons of the night were at me, terrifying my heart. I felt helpless to stop their assault. An idea came to me: *Get your cross necklace from your dresser and hold it.* I went to my dresser and then lay in bed, clutching the cross to my chest. I *was given* a prayer, a simple prayer that I repeated with each breath, "I believe in you."

As I prayed, I received the gift of the peace that passes understanding. I felt the presence of the Holy Spirit enter my being and softly buffet my wall of dread and doom. The wall did not crumble, but I was given a choice. I could focus upon and be consumed by my fears or trust in and focus on the One who said to his fear-gripped disciples: "I will ask the Father, and he will give you another Advocate, to be with you forever. This is the Spirit of truth, whom the world cannot receive, because it neither sees him nor knows him. You know him, because he abides with you, and he will be in you" (John 14:16-17). That night I received the gift of trusting God and coming to know God in a deeper, more intimate, and communal way. I felt strangely blessed.

How has such a gift of faith impacted my pastoral ministry? It has taught me that both my life and ministry are too over-whelming to live alone; and, in fact, I don't have to do so. It has showed me that the Spirit of truth is both with me and in me: in the loving faces of others and in the need to be with others in love. I have been showed that God's spirit is in me in depths beyond my comprehension. I know anew that "The Spirit helps us in our weakness; for we do not know how to pray as we ought, but that very Spirit intercedes with sighs too deep for words" (Rom. 8:26). This faith has showed me that meaning in life and in ministry is rooted in and flows from the mystery of faith, which the world can neither give nor take away from me. It has showed me that blessed living and ministry flow only from my poverty of spirit (see Matt. 5:3). I have come to realize my utter dependence on the One who longs for us and for whom we long.

The Gift of Being Tested

Jesus' Spirit of truth comes not only to offer us faith and the peace that passes understanding. This Spirit of truth also comes to show us the hidden condition of our hearts and to ask us to make critical choices about our hearts' deepest and often buried intentions. For many years now my dreams have been the arena through which the Spirit comes to reveal and test my heart. One of my recent dreams deeply affected my life and ministry.

In the dream, I am sitting by a window in the study hall of my high school. I am watching a female pastor who in her life has overcome serious health problems. She walks in front of the school to meet a gang of abusive, volatile men who verbally attack her and try to drive her away. She goes to them in a nonviolent and healing manner.

This same scene occurs on a daily basis for a period. I watch, and though not involved, I somehow feel connected to this healing woman and to the abusive men.

The woman leaves. A delegation from annual conference (the administrative structure of my denomination), who have clout and power, come into the study hall. As I sit by the window I feel that my heart is being given a choice: to align myself with this prestigious delegation or with the healing ministry the woman offers to the hostile men.

I subscribe to Jung's theory that places and people in dreams can represent parts of ourselves. I also believe the biblical and Jungian notion that God comes to us in our dreams. Through this dream God is showing me wounded parts of myself that I have denied and buried since my high school years. God is showing me that when pushed into a dark place in my heart, these parts may become abusive and dangerous. God further reveals that my long-held desire to seek worth and identity through professional success cannot come at the expense of neglecting the shadow parts of who I am—those parts that feel like the "unwanted me." And finally, God is giving me an angel of healing and light who, at some risk to herself, wants to bring peace, healing, and reconciliation to these separated parts.

I feel God is giving me both a most precious gift and a critical test through this dream. The gifts of divine mercy and healing embodied in the female pastor have come within reach of the unreachable, unwanted parts of me. God is giving me a new, expansive way to see who I am.

The test is this: Am I willing to love myself the way God longs to love me? Am I willing to let God love and make new the parts of me that I have been too afraid and ashamed to see, love, and own? Will I connect with the Spirit of truth's mysterious movement in my life? Or will I choose to forget what is happening behind the dream and pursue success in life through career achievements?

Through this dream, God gives no hint that career success is wrong to pursue. The pursuit becomes wrong only when I do it at the expense of denying the buried, broken parts of my heart that long for God's love. I feel graced that the Spirit is encouraging and aiding me to die to one way of seeing and living and to be born to a new one. "Very truly, I tell you, unless a grain of wheat falls into the earth and dies, it remains just a single grain; but if it dies, it bears much fruit" (John 12:24).

This test is a gift. It tells me that the key part of a pastoral ministry rooted in contemplative prayer is to do the inner work of discerning what the Spirit of truth is revealing to the contemplative's heart. I believe that contemplatives are called by God to do this work for their own well-being as well as for the well-being of others. Such encounters with the Spirit in the hidden places of the heart are a vital component in offering pastoral ministry rooted in contemplative prayer, and they clear the path for an awakening of the divine longing.

The Gift of Gratitude

I shall always carry with me the remembrance of the Sunday morning worship service following the tornado's destruction of a much-loved, 140-year-old, white-frame, small-town church. It was a bright July morning, and the spirit of the congregation was even brighter. We were grateful that we were alive! We were grateful that we were together in worship. The words that came to me as I led were, "We have grief, but there is a joy beneath our grief. Let's share our joys." And that's exactly what the congregation did.

The devastating tornado, followed by this uplifting worship service, was another experience with *strange blessings*; facing cancer was the first. I use that term because of what cancer brought into my life: the faith and renewed acquaintance with the Spirit of truth I mentioned earlier. The strange but very real blessing I encountered after the tornado was the spirit of gratitude's sudden appearance in my heart. This development surprised, bemused, and comforted me, because at heart I have never experienced myself as a grateful and positive person. I have always carried a certain grimness and despair about life and a covetousness about the good fortunes of others. Today I am not divorced completely from despair and jealousy, but I find myself being given a love and joy deeper than and greater than my negative view of things. Through this, Mr. Grim is slowly becoming Mr. Grateful!

What has occasioned these wonderful experiences in such dark moments? The psalmist furnishes us with a prayerful, poetic answer: "Because your steadfast love is better than life, my lips will praise you. / So I will bless you as long as I live; I will lift up my hands and call on your name" (Ps. 63:3-4). God's steadfast love, which is better than life, has occasioned these times of grace. The divine longing, steadfast amidst tornadoes, cancer, and a grim heart, gives my congregation and me this spirit of gratitude.

This spirit of gratitude is transforming the way I see and

offer ministry. Recently I was discussing the book *The Cloud of Unknowing* with two other clergy friends. One of them drew our attention to the author's reflections on Luke's story of Mary and Martha. All three of us practice contemplative prayer, so we appreciated the author's reflection and Jesus' defense of Mary against her sister's attack on her: "Martha, Martha, you are worried and distracted by many things; there is need of only one thing. Mary has chosen the better part, which will not be taken away from her" (Luke 10:41-42).

We all felt affirmed in our taking time to sit in contemplative prayer while many pastoral tasks demanded our attention. We also acknowledged that tasks were important, and Jesus was not attacking Martha's productivity but her being distracted by it from something of deep potency. The conversation pushed deeper and I asked, "But what exactly is Mary contributing to others by simply sitting before Jesus, being absorbed in him and what he has to say? What exactly are we contributing to others and our church by doing the same thing?" One woman responded, "I think through contemplation we discover the joy, gratitude, love, and peace to be found in simply taking the time to be with Jesus, without any agenda." That struck a chord with us. We talked of a need in our hearts to know holy joy, thankfulness, love, and peace. Our high-tech, got-to-keep-up culture, and obsessed-with-numbers church have lost their capacity for and understanding of the need to be with God simply for the sake of enjoying God and being grateful. We get lost and stressed; tasks lose their meaning without times of being with God in joy and gratitude.

This year in particular I have noted the important role Eucharist plays in both Luke and John's Easter stories. Eucharist means "thankfulness." Does not all ministry flow from Jesus'

Eucharist? Isn't Christ's ministry rooted in and defined by holy gratitude? Can ministry be ministry without it?

I am slowly awakening to the fact that before ministry is a task to be done, it is an act of gratitude to be offered in heart, mind, and spirit. Yes, we are called to the tasks of feeding the sheep in a needy world, but when we do this without taking time to enjoy the presence of Jesus as Mary did, we become like Martha—"worried and distracted by many things"—while missing the one thing needful. That one thing is rooted in responding to the divine longing.

The Gift of Community

I awakened about 7:30 the morning after the tornado. At first I did not want to get up. I felt alone and overwhelmed. As I lay there in that state, I overheard my daughter-in-law talking with a pastor friend from Fond du Lac. She had called to express concern and offer help. Overhearing this conversation, I heard a voice within utter a deep truth: *I am not alone.*

The days, the weeks, and the months since the tornado proved that the voice was correct. Other calls poured in. (My son and daughter-in-law were phone secretaries for days!) Cards and personal financial gifts came from friends. Volunteers from sister congregations, adjoining towns, and even prisoners flooded our village to help with the cleanup. Offers to help as well as financial donations totalling over $140,000 came to the church.

One morning recently I listened to a report on NPR's "Morning Edition" about Texas City, Texas. April 16, 1997, was the fiftieth anniversary of the explosion of a shop in the town's harbor. That disaster set a record in our nation for lives lost, and that record still stands. However, a woman recalling this event commented, "It is strange to say, but the disaster has made us a better town. Racial barriers came down. We are a closer-knit community because of that explosion." I hear people from my church and community utter the same sentiment about the effects of the tornado. People like us who have experienced a disaster have received a gift, the gift of divine grace. People like us have been given a glimpse into the eternal truth of God: We are not alone! At such moments we come to know that the reign of God is within us, around us, and beyond us. The good news I heard was that Christ was present. Christ was there in a caring pastor's phone call and in my poverty of spirit, helping me to see the caring community that surrounded me.

I felt a deep need both to share this truth and to express my personal gratitude and the gratitude of my congregation to the pastors and congregations of the Wisconsin Annual Conference of the United Methodist Church. I wanted to thank them for their care and financial support, and I wanted to say a word about being connected in a time of much disconnection within our church. I wrote a letter that appeared in the Wisconsin Conference magazine *Window*. My letter ended this way:

> I would like to conclude by switching roles from being pastor of Oakfield/Eden UM Parish to member of the Wisconsin Conference. We lay claim to being a connectional system. We feel quite often the breakdowns of this connectional system. But from the experience of this tornado, I have been given to see, "see" as in revelation of grace, that we are connected in Christ. The divine dimension of our "connectional system" is still intact, still operational, still filled with abundant love.
>
> Sometimes it does take a tornado to convince us, at least me, "that neither death, nor life, nor angels, nor rulers, nor things present, nor things to come, nor powers, nor height, nor depth, nor anything else in all creation [includ-

ing our cynicism about being connected], will be able to separate us from the love of God in Christ Jesus, our Lord."

This truth lives beneath the violence, differences, and disagreements that wrack our world and our church. I believe that one of the tasks and contributions of contemplative prayer is to constantly, in prayer and in community, remember this truth. For God knows all of us often forget it.

The late Henri Nouwen wrote eloquently in his book *In the Name of Jesus* of the contribution that the practice of contemplative prayer can make in today's church and world—how it can even enhance the gift of community. He reminded his readers that the original meaning of the word *theology* was "union with God in prayer." He then wrote of theology's need to reclaim its contemplative dimension.

> I have the impression that many of the debates within the Church around issues such as the papacy, the ordination of women, the marriage of priests, homosexuality, birth control, abortion, and euthanasia take place on a primarily moral level. On that level, different parties battle about right or wrong. But that battle is often removed from the experience of God's first love, which lies at the base of all human relationships. Words like right-wing, reactionary, conservative liberal, and left-wing are used to describe people's opinions, and many discussions then seem more like political battles for power than spiritual searches for the truth.
>
> Through the discipline of contemplative prayer, Christian leaders have to learn to listen again and again to the voice of love and to find there the wisdom and courage to address whatever issue presents itself to them. Dealing with burning issues without being rooted in a

deep personal relationship with God easily leads to divi-
siveness because, before we know it, our sense of self is
caught up in our opinion about a given subject.[1]

I do not put forth this contribution of contemplative prayer as
the answer to all that divides. However, contemplative prayer is
the door Christ gives us through which we walk to find
answers. I find it to be a crucial door. When I take the time in
prayer to realize the oneness Christ continually affords us, I may
not change my mind about my convictions. However, I do
change my mind about the way I see and speak my convictions. Most importantly, the way I see others changes when
contemplative prayer reminds me that we are one in Christ,
and the gift of community glows even brighter.

A Concluding Word

Frederick Buechner entitled the last book in his autobiographi-
cal trilogy *Telling Secrets*. Throughout my book, I have been
attempting to tell a secret, one that was showed me through
contemplative prayer. It is the secret of where the heart longs to
go. It is the secret that I believe God's Son Jesus came to reveal:
All of us carry the desire to go to the land of God's unspeakable blessing, where we live out together the primary desire of
our hearts: to be that unspeakable blessing to God and one
another. Nothing less will do; to be anything else is to betray
who and whose we are. And this is where the divine longing
finally leads us: where our deepest heart longs to go, in the
word images of my dream, the blue-hued valley of God's
shalom.

THE PASTORAL INTERVIEW

I share with you the process of the pastoral interview so you can use it in your own ministry if you choose. Before you begin, realize that this process occurs by invitation of the Holy Spirit only. By that I mean that the questions have come as a result of prayer; a pastor or other minister should feel led by God before asking a person to participate in an interview; and the interview itself must be rooted in a time of initial prayer. I say this because what one discovers and shares therein are the holy moments and places of another person's life and heart. In my experience many people hunger for this kind of in-depth conversation with a pastor, a spiritual leader, or a trusted spiritual friend; but one must treat this relationship and discovery with discretion and in confidence. Trust, though, that if you feel invited by the Holy Spirit to do this, you can share a deep gift of ministry.

The setting should be a quiet, private, and attractive place. I sometimes have quiet chant music playing. Once the interviewee has arrived, I begin the process, which takes between an hour and a half and two hours. I've interviewed about forty men and women so far. For this example let's say I'm interviewing a woman. After we visit briefly I would

1. Share a scripture passage. I most often use John 21, which includes Christ's communing with his disciples and commissioning Peter around the question, "Do you love me?" I read the passage and ask what stands out to her, and I share what strikes me. We conclude this first phase with prayer.

2. Describe the intention of the interview. I explain that this is a Sabbath time, a time for the woman to get in touch with her life path and instances when she has felt God's presence. I tell her that she will uncover what God leads her to uncover. I will not force her to reveal anything she's uncomfortable revealing.

3. Describe the process. I give the interviewee a piece of 8 1/2 x 11-inch paper and ask her to turn it horizontally. In the middle of the extreme left side of the sheet, I ask her to place a dot and to put her birth date below the dot. Across the sheet on the right side, I instruct her to write today's date. Then I tell her that she will do the following by herself:

- List all of the homes she has lived in, including addresses and dates. I tell her this will open a flood of memories.

- Create a memory flow by noting on the bottom of the page, the memories associated with the places she's lived. It is important to let the memories flow as long as they keep coming—allow even painful memories to come. All memories are part of her life fabric and hence are important.

- Walk through the memories and choose or be chosen by those memories that are significant turning points or stepping stones. Look for six to twelve such turning points.

- Chart the turning points between the two dots, making a life map. Add an initial or symbol for each turning point.

- Recall those times when she felt close to God, times that were holy moments. (Holy moments may or may not be turning points.) Add these to her life path.

I then leave her alone to do this exercise.

4. *Hear the interviewee's story.* When we come back together, I ask the woman to share the turning points with me chronologically. I listen and let myself be drawn into her story, making observations that strike me. I also ask questions for information or questions that might challenge her to look more deeply at something. It is crucial to be nonjudgmental and pass up the temptation to do psychological analysis or offer unrequested advice. Listen with humility, honor, openness, and a willingness to let the Spirit lead you and the person in what will become more a conversation than an interview. Then I ask her to share her holy moments.

5. *Conclude.* I ask what this time has meant to the interviewee and talk about the experience. I express gratitude for her time and the gift she has given me by allowing me this glimpse into her life. If it seems appropriate, I offer a prayer.

NOTES

Introduction

1. John Biersdorf, "The Minister as Contemplative," *Haelen* ix, no. 1 (summer 1989): 9–13.

2. Ibid.

3. Ibid., 11.

Chapter One

1. Macrina Wiederkehr, *A Tree Full of Angels* (San Francisco: Harper & Row, 1988), xi.

2. Paul Tillich, *The Shaking of the Foundations* (New York: Charles Scribner's, 1948), 162.

Chapter Two

1. John S. Dunne, *The Reasons of the Heart* as cited in *A Guide to Prayer for Ministers and Other Servants* by Rueben P. Job and Norman Shawchuck (Nashville, Tenn.: The Upper Room, 1983), 1769–77.

2. James Finley, *Merton's Palace of Nowhere* (Notre Dame, Ind.: Ave Maria Press, 1988), 29.

3. George Buttrick, ed., *Interpreter's Dictionary of the Bible* 2 (Nashville, Tenn.: Abingdon Press, 1962), 549–50.

Chapter Three

1. The Works of John Wesley V, sermon XXIV, discourse IV (Grand Rapids, Mich.: Zondervan Publishing House), 294–95.

2. The Works of John Wesley 18, ed. by W. Reginald Ward and Richard P. Heitzenrater (Nashville, Tenn.: Abingdon Press, 1988), 242–43.

3. Ibid., 243.

4. Ibid., 244

5. Ibid., 244–45.

6. Ibid., 245.

7. Ibid., 245–46.

8. Ibid., 247.

9. Ibid., 248–49.

10. Ibid., 249–50.

11. Ibid., 244–45.

12. Merton, *Contemplative Prayer* (New York: Doubleday, Image Book, 1968), 25.

13. The Works of Wesley 5, sermon XVII (Abingdon), 202–203.

14. Ibid., sermon XVI, 185.

15. Ibid., sermon XXIV, 295.

16. Merton, *Contemplative Prayer*, 107-108.

17. *John Wesley's Fifty-three Sermons*, ed. Edward H. Sugden (Nashville, Tenn.: Abingdon Press, 1983), 274.

18. Steve Harper, *Devotional Life in the Wesleyan Tradition* (Nashville, Tenn: The Upper Room, 1983), 22.

19. The Works of John Wesley 5 (Zondervan), 3.

20. Harper, *Devotional Life*, 31.

21. *John Wesley*, ed. by Albert Outler (New York: Oxford University Press, 1964), 333.

22. The Works of John Wesley III, sermon 101 (Abingdon), 430.

23. Ibid. I, sermon 27, discourse 7:608.

24 CD-Rom Works 30. The Works of John Wesley, 144.

25. Harper, *Devotional Life*, 61–62.

Chapter Four

1. James Finley, *The Awakening Call* (Notre Dame, Ind.: Ave Maria Press, 1986), 62.

2. Rueben P. Job, an unpublished paper. Used by permission.

3. Finley, *Merton's Palace of Nowhere*, 27.

4. Ibid.

5. Finley, *The Awakening Call*, 68.

6. Ibid.

7. Merton, *Contemplative Prayer*, 33.

8. Kathleen Norris, *Dakota: A Spiritual Geography* (New York: Ticknor & Fields, 1993), 197.

9. Ibid.; 198, 198–99.

10. Wesley Covenant Prayer, *The United Methodist Hymnal* (Nashville, Tenn.: The United Methodist Publishing House, 1989), 607.

Chapter Five

1. Norris, *Dakota*, 202.

2. Ibid., 203.

Chapter Six

1. Finley, *The Awakening Call*, 28.

Chapter Seven

1. Finley, *The Awakening Call*, 90.

2. Frederick Buechner, *The Sacred Journey* (SanFrancisco: Harper & Row, 1982), 68.

3. Ibid., 93.

Chapter Nine

1. Henri J. M. Nouwen, *In the Name of Jesus* (New York: The Crossroad Publishing Co., 1989), 30–31.